# NATIONAL GEOGRAPHIC
## KiDS

ADVENTURE

# EXPLORE!
## WORKBOOK

ages 5-6

# K

## kindergarten

National Geographic
Washington, D.C.

# This book belongs to:

**First Name:**

**Last Name:**

Since 1888, the National Geographic Society has funded more than 14,000 research, conservation, education, and storytelling projects around the world. National Geographic Partners distributes a portion of the funds it receives from your purchase to National Geographic Society to support programs including the conservation of animals and their habitats. To learn more, visit natgeo.com/info.

For more information, visit nationalgeographic.com, call 1-877-873-6846, or write to the following address:

National Geographic Partners, LLC
1145 17th Street NW
Washington, DC 20036-4688 U.S.A.

More for kids from National Geographic:
natgeokids.com

National Geographic Kids magazine inspires children to explore their world with fun yet educational articles on animals, science, nature, and more. Using fresh storytelling and amazing photography, Nat Geo Kids shows kids ages 6 to 14 the fascinating truth about the world—and why they should care. natgeo.com/subscribe

For rights or permissions inquiries, please contact National Geographic Books Subsidiary Rights: bookrights@natgeo.com

Cover design by Eva Absher-Schantz
Cover illustration by Melanie Mikecz
Interior illustration by Six Red Marbles

Trade paperback ISBN: 978-1-4263-7675-7

The publisher would like to thank Dr. Jan Esteraich, expert reviewer, and Katherine Kling, fact-checker. Book team: Katharine Moore, senior editor; Lori Epstein, photo manager; Six Red Marbles, writing, fact-checking, production; and Lauren Sciortino and David Marvin, associate designers.

Printed in China
24/RRDH/1

# Dear Parents and Caregivers,

These interactive pages teach the academic skills kids need to succeed in kindergarten, while focusing on favorite topics that will keep them engaged and excited as they learn. In these chapters, we explore themes associated with the natural world and everyday life, from rainforests and deserts to bugs, baby animals, and dinosaurs. Your child will be introduced to the most common kindergarten academic standards in true Nat Geo Kids style: through bold photos of nature, fun facts, jokes, and more.

To use this book, read through each theme-based spread with your child. Work with them to answer the questions and, as they progress, encourage independent problem-solving. Kid-friendly activities, such as connect-the-dots, mazes, and matching, make learning fun. Drawing, coloring, and writing activities help refine your child's fine motor skills. Each chapter covers the different content areas and early concepts your child will encounter at school, from math, reading, and writing, to sorting, colors, and the natural sciences. This integrated approach exposes your child to STEM concepts across multiple curriculum subjects, laying the groundwork for a lifelong love of science and exploration.

You can do the activities in any order you choose. If you go in order, your child will be introduced to the letters of the alphabet and numbers 1 through 10 in the first few chapters. As you do each activity, notice the skill label listed above it. If you feel your child needs more practice with a particular skill, visit the skills index at the back of the book on pages 250–252. It lists all the activities where you can practice that skill with your child. It organizes the activities by skill, such as letters, math, reading, writing, and early concepts.

At the end of each chapter, your child has a chance to reflect on their learning and take part in fun drawing, coloring, and counting activities. Once your child completes all the chapters, you can celebrate their accomplishment by awarding them the certificate at the end of the book. Together, you'll explore a great big world of learning!

# Table of Contents

CHAPTER 1: Under the Sea . . . . . . . . . . . . . . . . . 6

CHAPTER 2: In the Rainforest . . . . . . . . . . . . . 30

CHAPTER 3: Desert Fun . . . . . . . . . . . . . . . . . . 54

CHAPTER 4: School Days . . . . . . . . . . . . . . . . . 80

CHAPTER 5: All the Senses . . . . . . . . . . . . . . . 106

CHAPTER 6: Bugs and Friends . . . . . . . . . . . 132

CHAPTER 7: Baby Animals . . . . . . . . . . . . . . 160

CHAPTER 8: Dino Days . . . . . . . . . . . . . . . . . 184

CHAPTER 9: On the Move . . . . . . . . . . . . . . . 212

Answer Key . . . . . . . . . . . . . . . . . . . . . . . . . . 240

Skills Index . . . . . . . . . . . . . . . . . . . . . . . . . . 250

Photo Credits . . . . . . . . . . . . . . . . . . . . . . . 253

Award Certificate . . . . . . . . . . . . . . . . . . . . 256

# CHAPTER 1

This is a parrotfish. It has about a thousand tiny teeth in its mouth!

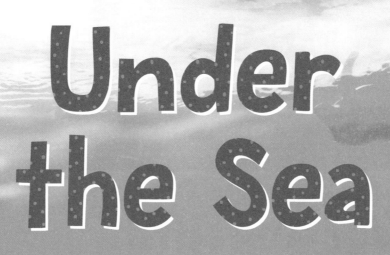

# Under the Sea

**Come explore the ocean!** In this chapter, you'll dive deep to discover more about life under the sea. What sea creatures would you like to see in person one day?

# Beautiful Angelfish

Angelfish come in lots of different colors and patterns.
They all have flat bodies and tiny mouths.

**LETTERS**  **WRITING**

## A is for Angelfish

**Trace and then write A and a. Say the sound of the
letters as you trace and write them.**

A a A a A a A a A a

**MATH**  **WRITING**

## Time to Eat!

**How many sea sponges is the angelfish eating? Trace and write
the number 1.**

1 1 1

# Find the One

**Can you count the fish? Color each fish that has the number 1 inside.**

A Halo!

# Bubble Up!

Pufferfish can do something amazing. They puff up into a ball shape so predators can't eat them!

**MATH** | **WRITING**

## Double Bubble

**Circle where you see 2 bubbles stuck together. Then trace and write the number 2.**

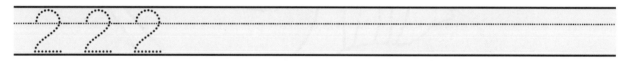

# Ready to Pop!

**Color the bubbles with the letters B or b.**

E B p b k B

# B is for Bubbles

**Trace and then write B and b. Say the sound of the letters as you trace and write them.**

Pufferfish taste bad to other fish.

Bb Bb Bb Bb Bb

# Colorful Coral

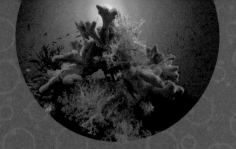

Corals are tiny living creatures. Many corals together make up a coral reef. Coral reefs are home to many plants and animals.

**LETTERS** **WRITING**

## C is for Coral

**Trace and then write C and c. Say the sound of the letters as you trace and write them.**

CcCcCcCcCcCc

**EARLY CONCEPTS**

## Pretty Patterns

**Look at the patterns. Circle what comes next.**

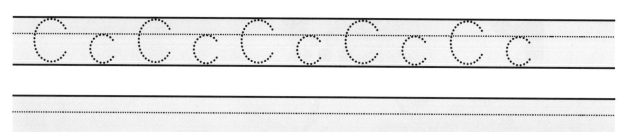

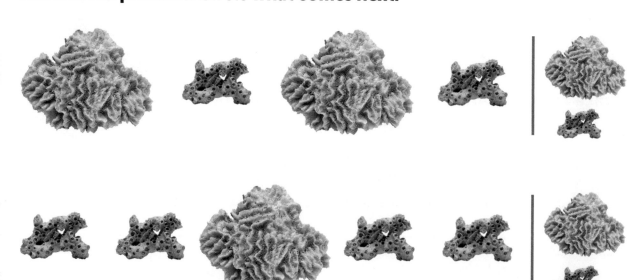

# Find the Corals

We are on an underwater expedition to find corals!

**Find and circle:**

- **the coral that is in the cave**
- **the coral that is by the fish**

# See the Clownfish!

**Find 3 clownfish in the coral reef!**
**Trace and then write the number 3.**

# Clever Dolphins

Dolphins are smart. They talk to one another using clicks and squeaks. They also jump and splash to communicate!

**LETTERS** | **WRITING**

## D is for Dolphin

**Trace and then write D and d. Say the sound of the letters as you trace and write them.**

D d D d D d D d D d D d

**MATH** | **WRITING**

## Nosedive!

**Count 4 dolphins. Then trace and write the number 4.**

Bottlenose dolphins can leap as high as 20 feet (6 m) in the air!

4 4 4

# What Starts With D?

Other animal names have the same beginning sound as dolphin.

**Circle the animal names that start with d.**

deer

tiger

dog

lizard

parrot

duck

# Slippery Eels

Eels are fish that look like snakes! Many eels hide in the mud during the day. They come out at night to look for food.

**Some eels can grow to be nearly 12 feet (3.7 m) long!**

**LETTERS** **WRITING**

## E is for Eel

**Trace and then write E and e. Say the sound of the letters as you trace and write them.**

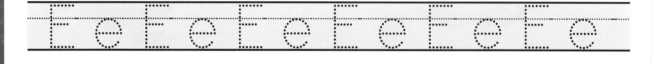

**MATH** **WRITING**

## Fab Fives

**Count the sea star's arms. Then trace and write the number 5.**

# Wiggly Fives

Count and circle **5** eels in each group.

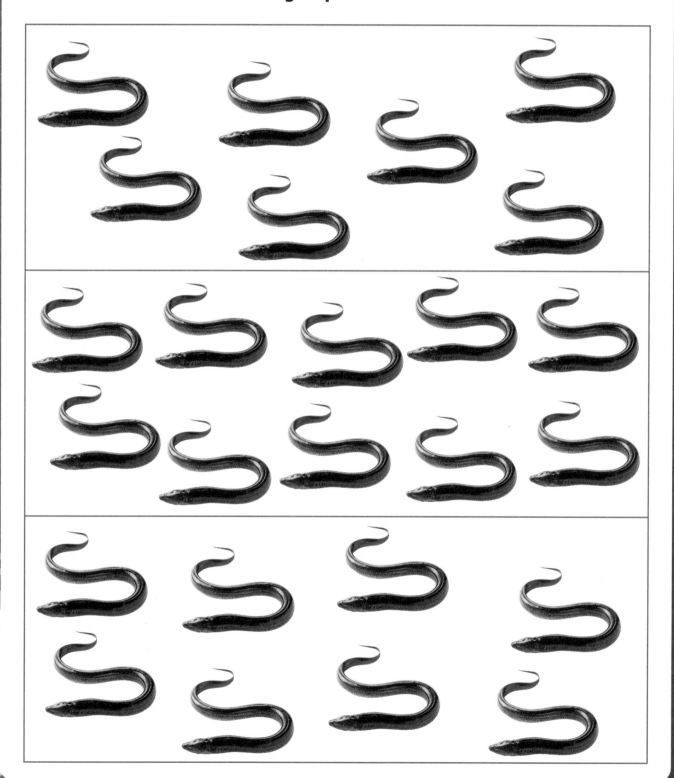

# Fish in the Reef

The Great Barrier Reef in Australia is the largest coral reef in the world! It is home to thousands of kinds of plants and animals.

**LETTERS**  **WRITING**

## F is for Fish

**Trace and then write F and f. Say the sound of the letters as you trace and write them.**

F F F F F F F F F F F

**MATH**  **WRITING**

## Fish Find

**Circle the 6 fish hiding in the reef. Then trace and write the number 6.**

6 6 6

# Reef Maze

Help the fish get to the reef. Follow the letters **F** and **f**. Say the sound of the letter each time you see **F** or **f**.

# A Great Big Ocean

Ocean water covers most of Earth. Some parts of the ocean are miles deep! Almost all of Earth's water is in the ocean.

**EARLY CONCEPTS**

## Around the Globe

A globe is a map of Earth in the shape of a ball. On this globe, the letter L is on all the areas that are land. The letter O is on all the areas that are ocean.

**Color the land green.**
**Color the ocean blue.**

Only a tiny part of the ocean has been explored!

# G is for Globe

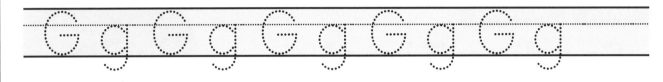

Trace and then write **G** and **g**. Say the sound of the letters as you trace and write them.

# Hidden Turtles

The ocean is so big! It can be a great place to hide.

**Find the 7 sea turtles hiding in this picture. Then trace and write the number 7.**

# Enormous Humpbacks

A humpback whale can weigh as much as 20 cars!
These giant creatures eat tiny animals called krill.

**MATH** **WRITING**

## Feeding Time!

**Find 8 krill before the humpback whale snaps them up! Then trace and write the number 8.**

**LETTERS** **WRITING**

## H is for Humpback

**Trace and then write H and h. Say the sound of the letters as you trace and write them.**

H h H h H h H h H h H h

# Which One Belongs?

Humpbacks are ocean animals. They belong in the ocean with other ocean animals.

**Look at the first picture in each row. Which of the other pictures belongs with it? Circle it.**

Each humpback whale has a different pattern on its tail.

# Big and Small

Ocean animals come in all sizes. Blue whales are the largest animals on Earth. Zooplankton can be too small to see.

**EARLY CONCEPTS** | **MATH**

## Big or Small?

**Look at the animals in the picture below. Circle the big animals. Draw a square around the small animals.**

BLUE WHALE

# I is for Isopod

ISOPOD

An isopod is a small ocean creature that looks like a bug.

**Trace and then write I and i. Say the sound of the letters as you trace and write them.**

# Big Sharks

Sharks can be huge!

**Count 9 sharks. Then trace and write the number 9.**

# Floating Jellyfish

Jellyfish are not fish at all! They do not have bones like fish do.
Some jellyfish can sting with long body parts called tentacles.

**MATH** **WRITING**

## 10 Tentacles

**Count 10 tentacles!
Then trace and write
the number 10.**

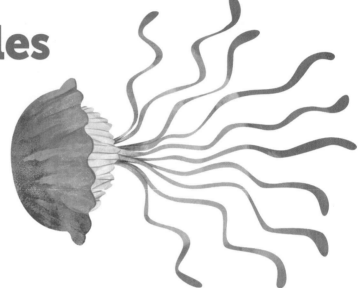

10 10 10

**LETTERS** **WRITING**

## J is for Jellyfish

**Trace and then write J and j. Say the sound of the letters as you trace
and write them.**

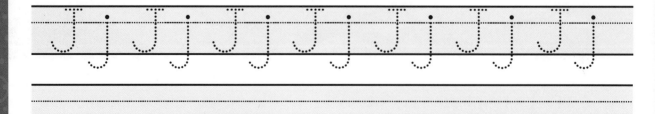

# What's Hiding?

There's an animal hiding on the ocean floor.

**Connect the dots in the right order from 1 to 10 to find it!**

# Ocean Adventure

Great job! You met some of the many creatures living in the deep blue sea. People discovered these animals by exploring the ocean. Ocean explorers can use machines called underwater drones to learn more about sea life.

Scientists can control these drones using remote controls.

# Be an Explorer

Imagine you are an ocean explorer.

**What creatures would you like to see? Draw them in the scene. Then have someone write down what you want to say about the creatures you drew.**

# CHAPTER 2

TOUCAN

When toucans sing, they sound like croaking frogs!

# In the Rainforest

**You're an explorer!** Get ready for a trip to the rainforest. Rainforests are home to lots of plants and animals. Many of them can't be found anywhere else in the world. Are you ready to meet these amazing creatures?

# Cute Kinkajous

The furry kinkajou uses its long tail to help it climb through the trees. It even snuggles with its tail when sleeping!

**LETTERS** | **WRITING**

## K is for Kinkajou

Trace and then write K and k. Say the sound of the letters as you trace and write them.

K K K K K K K K K K K K

**MATH**

## A Fig Feast

Kinkajous love figs!

**Count the number of figs on the tree branch.**

**How many figs did you find? Circle the correct number.**

3     4     5     6     7

# The Search for Figs

Follow the letters **K** and **k** to help the kinkajou find the fig tree. Say the sound of the letter each time you see **K** or **k**.

**Kinkajous stick their long tongues into beehives in search of honey!**

# Leaping Lemurs

Many lemurs spend their time in rainforest trees. These wide-eyed animals live mostly on the African island of Madagascar.

Lemurs have pads on their fingers and toes to help them grip tree trunks and branches.

**LETTERS** **WRITING**

## L is for Lemur

**Trace and then write L and l. Say the sound of the letters as you trace and write them.**

# Rainforest Friends

The lemur is just one animal whose name begins with the letter L.

**Draw a line from the L to each animal whose name begins with L.**

# So Many Monkeys!

Did you know that there are more than 300 types of monkeys on Earth? You might spot one swinging through rainforest trees.

**EARLY CONCEPTS**  **LETTERS**

## Where Am I?

Write an **M** on the monkey that is **in** the tree.
Write an **m** on the monkey that is **under** the tree.

**LETTERS**  **WRITING**

## M is for Monkey

Trace and then write **M** and **m**. Say the sound of the letters as you trace and write them.

M m M m M m M m

# A Monkey Meal

**What do monkeys like to eat? Connect the dots in the right order from 1 to 20 to find out.**

A A mon-key!

# Wake Up, It's Dark!

Some rainforest animals only come out at night. Bats and hedgehogs sleep all day. They look for food after sunset.

## Nighttime Rhyme

**Circle the pictures of things that rhyme with night.**

## N is for Nighttime

**Trace and then write N and n. Say the sound of the letters as you trace and write them.**

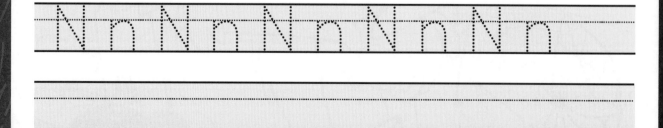

? **What are some things you like to do at night?**

# Day and Night!

**Write a D next to the pictures of daytime.**
**Write an N next to the pictures of nighttime.**

EARLY CONCEPTS

# In the Night Sky

**Circle the pictures of things you can see in the night sky.**

stars

sun

moon

# Oh, Okapi!

Meet the okapi! It may look a little like a zebra, but it's really related to the giraffe. Okapis use their long tongues to get food.

**LETTERS**  **WRITING**

## O is for Okapi

Trace and then write O and o. Say the sound of the letters as you trace and write them.

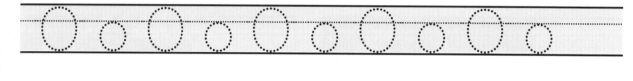

**READING**

## It's the Same Sound!

Say the word for each picture. Circle the ones that have a long o sound, like the long o in okapi.

# Leaf Math

Okapis eat leaves.

**There are 3 leaves. Draw 2 more. Then count the leaves. How many leaves are there now? Write the answer on the line.**

An okapi's tongue is long enough to clean its eyes and ears.

3 + 2 =

**There are 4 leaves. Draw 3 more. How many leaves are there now? Write the answer on the line.**

4 + 3 =

# Bright Birds

**Q** What is a parrot's favorite game? ↪

The rainforest is filled with many colorful birds. They soar through the air and perch on trees. Their sounds fill the forest!

**LETTERS** **WRITING**

## P is for Parrot

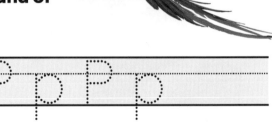

Trace and then write **P** and **p**. Say the sound of the letters as you trace and write them.

P p P p P p P p P p P p

**MATH** **WRITING**

## Sticking Together

How many parrots are on the branch? _____

# A Splash of Color!

**A** Hide-and-speak!

What color are these rainforest birds? Draw a line from the color to the bird that matches it.

Red

Orange

Yellow

Green

Blue

# Colorful Quetzal

Look at the long tail on that bird! It is a quetzal. The male has much longer tail feathers than the female.

**READING**  **WRITING**

## Words to Know

**Trace the words on the quetzal's feathers.**

**LETTERS**  **WRITING**

## Q is for Quetzal

**Trace and then write Q and q. Say the sound of the letters as you trace and write them.**

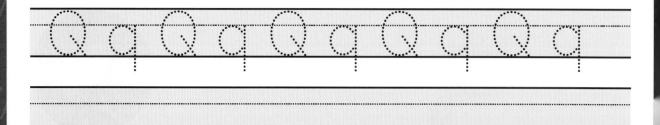

# Color Me Perfect!

Color the quetzal. Color the parts with an uppercase Q green.
Color the parts with a lowercase q red.

**?** What other animals can you think of that are red or green?

# Rainforest Rainbows

Rainforests get lots of rain! Have you ever seen a rainbow after a rainstorm? Rainbows happen when sunlight hits drops of water.

**LETTERS**  **WRITING**

## R is for Rain

**Trace and then write R and r. Say the sound of the letters as you trace and write them.**

RrRrRrRrRrRrRrRrRr

**READING**

## Where's the Rain?

Some words are made up of two smaller words.

**Find the word rain in each word below and underline it.**

rainforest

rainbow

raindrop

# What Happens Next?

A storm comes. It rains. You see a rainbow!

**Put the pictures in order. Write 1 next to what comes first.**
**Write 2 next to what comes next. Write 3 next to what comes last.**

# Sssssnakes!

Many kinds of snakes live in the rainforest. Snakes have tough, dry plates called scales that cover their bodies and protect them.

## What Begins With S?

**Say the name of each picture.**
**Circle the things that start with S.**

## S is for Snake

**Trace and then write S and s. Say the sound of the letters as you trace and write them.**

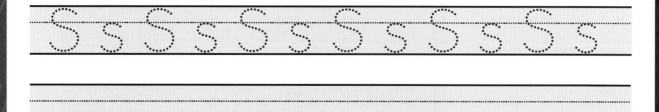

# Snake Shapes

Snakes can move in so many ways!

**Color the snakes that are in the shape of an S.**

# Hop, Tree Frog!

Tree frogs have pads on their feet that help them climb. They hop, too. The red-eyed tree frog can jump more than 5 feet (1.5 m).

**LETTERS**  **WRITING**

## T is for Tree Frog

**Trace and then write T and t. Say the sound of the letters as you trace and write them.**

**MATH**  **WRITING**

## Fly, Fly, Fly!

This tree frog catches 3 flies at a time for a tasty meal.

**Circle groups of 3 flies for the tree frog to eat. How many groups of 3 are there?**

There are _____ groups of 3.

# Hop to It!

Help the tree frog find its way across the water. Follow the words you and me. Say each word when you find it.

**Q** What did the bus driver say to the tree frog?

**A** "Hop on!"

# Thanks, Rainforest!

Here are some more amazing plants and animals you might see in a rainforest.

jaguar

poison dart frog

tapir

passionflower

orchid

water lily

# Keep Learning!

Draw a picture of something in the rainforest that you'd like to know more about. What questions do you have? Ask someone to write them below your drawing.

# CHAPTER 3

The roadrunner runs more than it flies. This speedy bird can run up to 17 miles an hour (27 km/h)!

# Desert Fun

**Deserts get very little rain.** They can be hard places for plants and animals to live. But lots of plants and animals do make their homes there! As you read this chapter, look for ways living things stay alive in the desert.

# Under the Desert Sky

The sun can be very hot in some deserts. How do the animals stay cool? Many desert animals find shade under rocks or trees.

**LETTERS** **WRITING**

## U is for Under

Trace and then write **U** and **u**. Say the sound of the letters as you trace and write them.

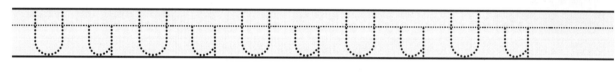

**EARLY CONCEPTS**

## Spot the Animals

Some of these animals are staying out of the sun.

**Circle the animals that are under something.**

# Stay Cool!

**What could you go under to stay in the shade?**
**Connect the dots in order from 1 to 30 to find out!**

A desert is a place that gets less than 10 inches (25 cm) of rain in a year.

# Very, Very Hot

Deserts are among the hottest places on Earth. The temperature in Death Valley, a desert in California, has reached over 130°F (54°C)!

**LETTERS** **WRITING**

## V is for Very Hot!

**Trace and then write V and v. Say the sound of the letters as you trace and write them.**

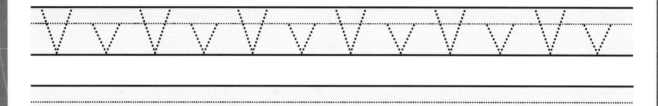

**EARLY CONCEPTS**

## Hold That Water

A cactus holds water inside itself to survive in the hot desert. Even with very little water, cactuses can grow very large.

**Which cactus is largest? Circle it.**

# Ready for the Journey

**?** What would you bring along if you were traveling across the desert?

When you walk across the desert, you need to carry all of your gear with you, including water!

**Which bag or container would hold more?**
**Circle the one in each row that holds more.**

# Desert Wonder

An oasis is a special place in the desert where there is enough water for plants to grow. The water is underground!

**LETTERS** **WRITING**

## W is for Wonder

**Trace and then write W and w. Say the sound of the letters as you trace and write them.**

W w W w W w W w

**READING**

## What Does It Start With?

lizard

**Name each picture. Circle the pictures that start with W.**

fox

wind

cactus

wing

# Shadow Match

The sun creates big shadows in the desert.

**Draw a line to match each desert dweller to its shadow.**

A desert oasis gives travelers a place to rest and find water and shade.

# Underground Worlds

Some animals stay cool in the desert by digging underground homes. It's cooler under the sandy soil!

**WRITING**

## Where's Your Home?

These desert animals have underground homes.

**Trace the name of each animal.**

badger

mouse

EARLY CONCEPTS

# "X" It Out

**Put an X on the things that don't belong in the desert.**

octopus

fish

camel

cactus

lizard

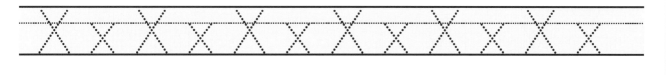
whale

LETTERS  **WRITING**

A Squeakers!

# X is in Excellent!

**X marks the spot! Trace and then write X and x. Say the sound of the letters as you trace and write them.**

X X X X X X X X X X X X

# The Lovely Yucca

Yucca plants live in the desert. You can count their leaves to help tell their age. Some yucca plants in Nevada are 200 years old!

**READING** **WRITING**

## What Can You See?

**Trace the words in the sentence.**

I can see a big yucca plant.

**LETTERS** **WRITING**

## Y is for Yucca

**Trace and then write Y and y. Say the sound of the letters as you trace and write them.**

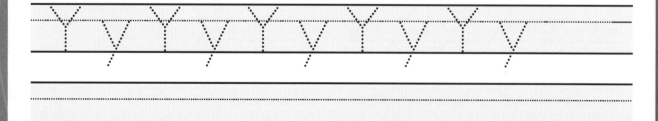

# How Many Leaves?

Count the leaves on the yucca plant. How many more leaves do you need to draw to get to **10**? Draw them on the plant. Color it.

Some yucca plants in the desert can grow taller than a giraffe!

The plant had _____ leaves.

I drew _____ more leaves to make 10.

# Zigzagging Lizards

What's that creature zipping across the sand? It's a lizard! Many lizards move in a zigzag pattern to escape danger.

**LETTERS** **WRITING**

## Z is for Zigzag

**Trace and then write Z and z. Say the sound of the letters as you trace and write them.**

**LETTERS**

## Catch Some Z's

**Circle the things that start with Z.**

zebra

cup

chair

zipper

**MATH**

# Home Sweet Home

**Help the lizard find its way home! Draw a line connecting the numbers in order from 1 to 20. The line can go in any direction.**

| | | | | | | | |
|---|---|---|---|---|---|---|---|
| 1 | 2 | 3 | 4 | 5 | 6 | 7 | 8 |
| 18 | 4 | 13 | 6 | 1 | 5 | 9 | 2 |
| 3 | 11 | 6 | 4 | 5 | 10 | 8 | 19 |
| 14 | 6 | 1 | 7 | 11 | 15 | 9 | 7 |
| 5 | 2 | 6 | 12 | 5 | 10 | 9 | 18 |
| 9 | 4 | 13 | 10 | 7 | 12 | 5 | 10 |
| 18 | 14 | 1 | 12 | 6 | 1 | 19 | 7 |
| 15 | 16 | 17 | 18 | 19 | 20 | | |

It's a very long tail!

**A**

# Sting, Scorpion!

Scorpions are famous for stinging with their tails. The venom in their sting helps them catch a meal and protect themselves.

## What's That Creature?

Connect the dots in order from **A** to **Z** to see what's hanging around in the desert. Then color the picture.

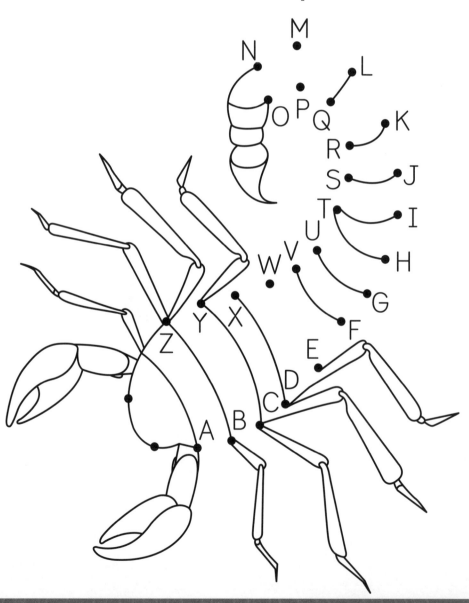

# Scorpion Shapes

Trace the shapes the scorpion made in the sand. Color the shapes with **3** sides red. Color the shapes with **4** sides blue.

Scorpions have lived on Earth since before the time of the dinosaurs!

# Size It Up!

Living things in the desert can be big or small. Some of the biggest things are also older. They have had more time to grow!

**EARLY CONCEPTS** | **MATH**

## Size Wise

Compare the sizes of living things in the desert.

1. Draw a triangle around the cactus that is **taller**.

2. Circle the snake that is **longer**.

3. Draw a square around the lizard that is **bigger**.

**?** What are the biggest plants and animals where you live?

# Small Words

Some words are small! You can learn them quickly.

**Trace and then write these small words.**

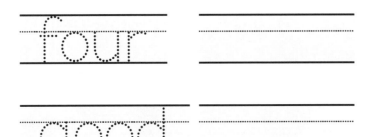

# Listen to the E

**The letters ea make the long e sound like in the word eat.**
**Which words below have that same sound? Circle them.**

heat          meat          beak

bed          pen          seat

# Desert Addition

Some animals in the desert live in groups. They can work together to find food and stay safe. There is strength in numbers!

These are meerkats. Sometimes they live in groups of up to 50!

# Do the Math

**Count the things that live in the desert. Add them together.**
**Write the answers on the lines.**

 = \_\_\_\_

 = \_\_\_\_

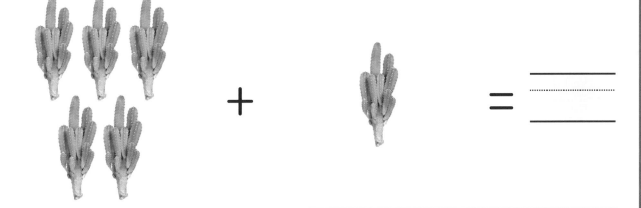 = \_\_\_\_

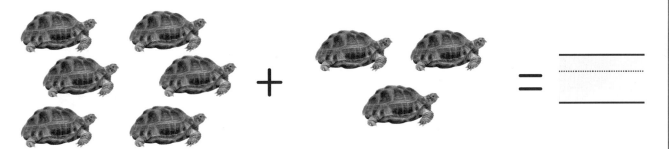 = \_\_\_\_

# Desert Plants

How can plants grow in the desert? Desert plants need very little water. Some can even hold water inside their leaves!

## Plants All Around

**Find the desert plants. Draw a line from each plant on the bottom of the page to the matching plant in the desert picture.**

**yucca**

**brittlebush shrub**

**prickly pear cactus**

**desert lily**

# Joshua Tree

One desert plant is called the Joshua tree.

**Place an X next to the things that start with J like Joshua tree.**

crayon

jar

pretzel

apple

spoon

juice

# Cold Deserts

**Q** Where does a penguin keep its money? →

Not all deserts are hot! Antarctica is the world's biggest desert. It gets very little rain or snow. Penguins live in this desert.

Antarctica

**EARLY CONCEPTS**     **READING**

## Tell About It

**Circle the words that tell about a cold desert. Put an X on the words that do not tell about a cold desert.**

hot          sandy          chilly

dry          icy          rainy

# Go Home, Penguin!

Oops! The penguin got lost and needs help getting home.

**Connect the pictures of things that start with P to help the penguin find its way through the maze.**

A In a snowbank!

77

# Desert Survivors

You learned a lot about life in the desert. It is not an easy place to live! But desert plants and animals have ways to get food and water. They know how to stay cool and safe.

This desert tortoise stays cool by sleeping underground.

**EARLY CONCEPTS**

## What Lives There?

**Circle the animals you learned about that live in the desert.**

# Survival Hero

**Think of an animal or plant you learned about in this chapter. Draw how it survives in the desert. Then color in your picture.**

# CHAPTER 4

# School Days

**Time for school!** Children all around the world learn in schools. In this chapter, you'll explore the fun you can have at school—from playtime to art, music, and story time!

In Bangladesh, some schools are on boats!

# Let's Go!

In many countries, children take a bus to school. School buses in the United States are often yellow. That makes the bus easy to see!

**EARLY CONCEPTS** | **MATH** | **WRITING**

## Red Shirt, Blue Shirt

Count the children on the school bus. Then answer the questions.

How many children have **red** shirts? _____

How many children have **blue** shirts? _____

Do more children have red shirts or blue shirts?     red     blue

# Letter the Way

Help the school bus find its way down the road! Fill in the missing letters on the path.

**A** At the buzz stop!

Q Why are fish so smart? →

# Learn and Play

School is a place to learn. Kids learn how to read, write, and count at school. They also play inside and outside.

**WRITING**

## See and Say

**Trace each word. Then write the word on the line.**

into

like

must

new

no

now

# B is the Best!

Bus begins with the letter B.

**Say the word for each picture. Draw a line from Bb to each word that begins with the b sound, as in bus.**

**A** They live in schools!

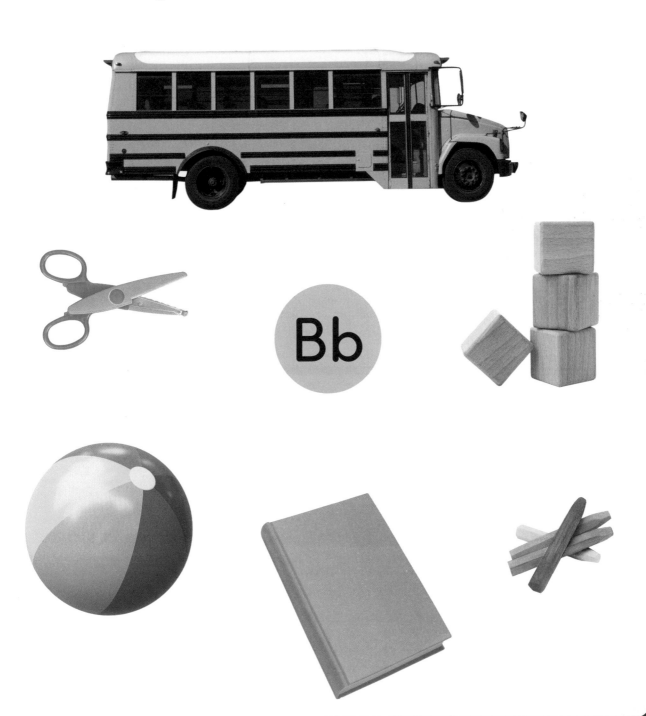

Bb

# Make New Friends

School is a place to meet friends. You may sit with friends in class or play with them on the playground. Friends make school fun!

**MATH** | **WRITING**

## Jump to It!

These friends missed a few numbers when they were counting.

**Write in the missing numbers.**

| 5 | 6 | | | |
|---|---|---|---|---|
| 10 | | | | 14 |

# Time to Share

Two friends are playing in their classroom.

**Add up the toys in each row to see how many they have all together.**

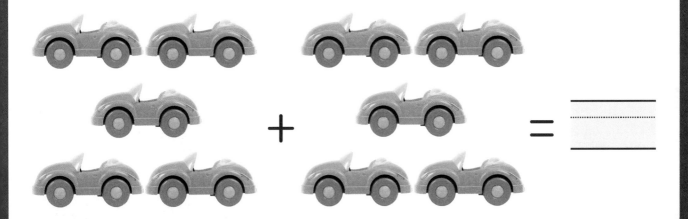

# Lunchtime!

? What is your favorite snack?

Many kids eat lunch at school. You can get your lunch at school or bring it from home. What do you usually eat for lunch?

**READING**

## Pick a P

Pizza begins with the letter P.

**Circle the other foods that begin with the same sound as pizza.**

# It's a Pizza Pie

Let's get ready to eat. How many slices of pizza are there?

_____
.................................
_____

Nan ate **2** slices of pizza. How many slices of pizza are left?

_____
.................................
_____

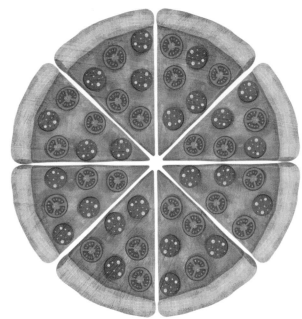

# A Piece of Pizza, Please!

Count the circles on each slice of pizza. Draw a square around the pizza with the most circles.

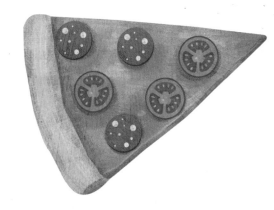

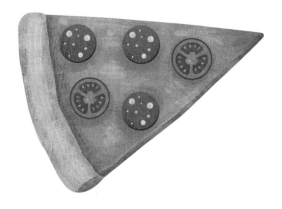

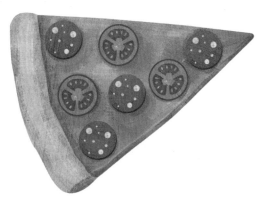

# Ants on a Log

You can make your own healthy snacks for school. Did you ever try ants on a log? Don't worry! They're not real ants. They're raisins!

**MATH** | **WRITING**

## It's Raining Raisins!

It's snack time at school!

**Count the raisins on each piece of celery. Write the number on the line.**

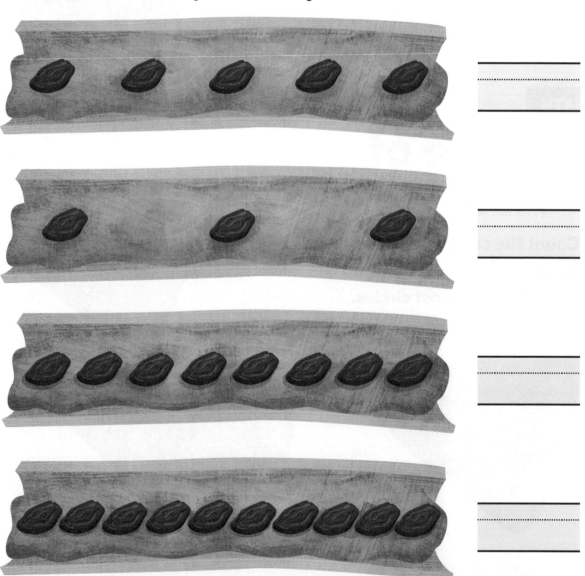

# Reading a Recipe

**Look at the recipe for ants on a log.**

**What You Need**

Raisins are dried grapes. It takes three or four days in the hot sun for a grape to become a raisin.

**What to Do**

Uh-oh! These steps are out of order!

**Write 1, 2, 3, and 4 on the lines to show the order of the steps.**

Add raisins.

Wash the celery.

Eat and enjoy!

Spread peanut butter on the celery.

# Super Subjects

There are many fun things to do at school, like making music and art! What art and music activities do you like best?

## Oh! It's an Oboe

An oboe is a musical instrument.

**Say oboe. Oboe begins and ends with the long o sound. Say the word for each picture. Circle the picture if you hear the long o sound.**

EARLY CONCEPTS

# Sort the Supplies

Help Mia and Adam find their supplies. Mia likes music. Adam likes art. Draw a line from each child to the things they need for their favorite activity.

Mia

Adam

A Moo-sic!

# Time for Art

Art is about making things. You can draw. You can paint. You can make shapes out of clay. And you can use a lot of colors!

## Refill the Paint Tray

This paint tray needs to be filled with more paint!

**Color each circle with the paint color shown.**

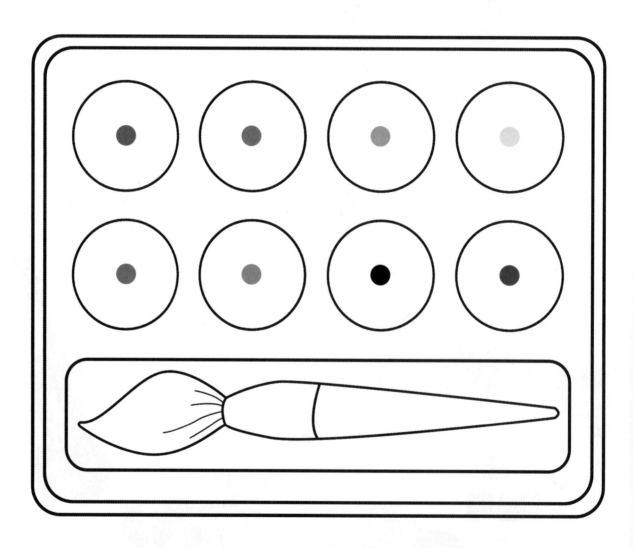

# Paint by Number

**Use the color code to color the picture.**

Paint colors can be made from berries, plants, and even ground-up rocks.

## Code

**1 - red**  **2 - blue**  3 - yellow  **4 - purple**  **5 - green**  6 - orange

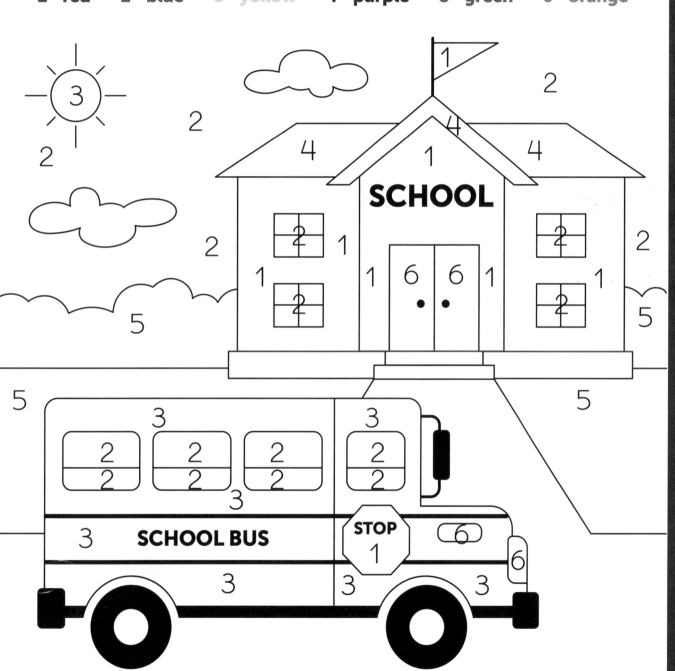

# Shape Up!

At school, you will learn about shapes. Some shapes are flat. Some shapes are solid. Take a look at these examples!

These shapes are flat.

These shapes are not flat. They are solids.

circle

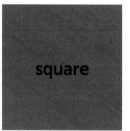
square

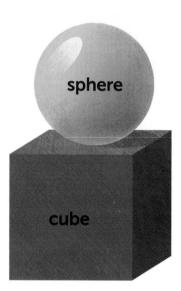
sphere

cube

**EARLY CONCEPTS**　　**LETTERS**　　**MATH**　　**WRITING**

# Flat or Solid?

Write **F** below the flat shapes. Write **S** below the solid shapes.

# Shapes and More Shapes

**Draw a shape on the line to complete each pattern.**

_____

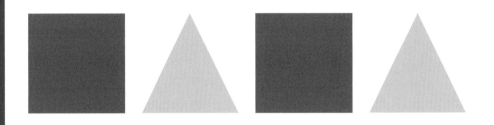

_____

_____

**Create your own pattern of shapes in the space below.**

# Party Time!

At school, you may celebrate special days. A party is a time to have fun as a class. What special days would you like to celebrate?

**EARLY CONCEPTS**  **MATH**

## Scoop It Up

Help scoop the ice cream into each cone!
Draw the correct number of scoops on each cone.

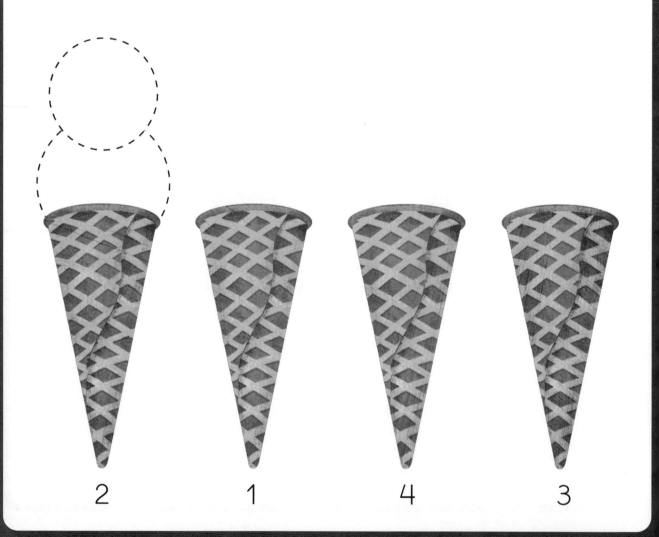

2    1    4    3

# Find the Party!

Follow the letter P through the maze to help the students find the party in their schoolyard. Say the sound of the letter P each time you find one.

It takes most people about 50 licks to eat one scoop of an ice-cream cone.

# A Place to Play

A fun part of the school day is playing outside on the playground with friends. What's your favorite thing to do on the playground?

**EARLY CONCEPTS** | **MATH** | **WRITING**

## Ball Count

Lots of people are playing with balls on the playground.

**Count all the balls you see.**

# There are _____ balls.

# Ready to Climb

**?** What games are people playing on the playground on the opposite page?

**What part of a playground has a ladder to climb?**
**Connect the dots in the right order from A to Z to find out.**

# A School Garden

Many schools have gardens. Students sometimes help plant seeds. They help water plants. What would you like to grow?

**EARLY CONCEPTS**

## Budding Buddies

These flowers are growing in the garden!

**Circle the flower that is tallest.**

# Along the Garden Path

Look at the letters written on this garden path.

**Some of them are missing! Fill in the missing letters.**

"Kindergarten" means "garden of children" in German.

# School's Out!

**Q** Where's the best place for kids to grow flowers? ↘→

You learned a lot about the things you'll see and do at school. What was your favorite part of the day?

**EARLY CONCEPTS**

## Your Turn

**Imagine you just spent a day at school. Draw yourself with a new friend! Write your name and your friend's name on your drawing.**

# School Words

Here are some words you'll use at school.

**Find and circle them in the word search.**
**Look for words across and down.**

A A kinder-garden!

| bus | school | books | art | play | math |

| X | G | E | B | W | P |
|---|---|---|---|---|---|
| S | C | H | O | O | L |
| M | B | W | O | D | A |
| A | R | T | K | G | Y |
| T | Z | C | S | A | E |
| H | B | U | S | R | O |

CHAPTER 5

# All the Senses

**How do we explore the world around us?** We use our senses! In this chapter, you'll learn about how people and animals see, hear, smell, taste, and touch the world around them.

**?** Picture yourself at the beach. What do you see? What do you hear? What do you smell?

# My Five Senses

Most people and animals have five senses. They are sight, hearing, smell, taste, and touch. What can you discover with your senses?

**EARLY CONCEPTS**

## Bear Sense

Draw a line from each word to the body part that allows this panda to see, hear, smell, taste, or touch.

The giant panda is one of the world's rarest animals. There are only about 1,800 living in the wild.

hear

taste

see

smell

touch

# Matching Senses

**Trace each sense word. Then draw a line from each word to the picture that shows that sense.**

 see

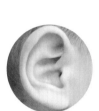 hear

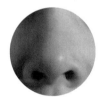 smell

 taste

 touch

# Can You See Me?

Do you like to play hide-and-seek? Some animals are very good at it! They blend in with the things around them.

## Where Are They?

**These animals are hiding. Can you see them? How do they hide?**
**Circle the colored word that describes what you see in each picture.**

**The stick bug is** on under **the stick.**

**The owl is** in above **the tree.**

**The fox is** under on **the snow.**

**The deer is** behind in front of **the tree.**

# Count Me In!

Some animals stay safe by living together.

**Count the animals in each picture.**

I see _____ elephants.

I see _____ meerkats.

I see _____ zebras.

I see _____ flamingos.

# Did You Hear That?

We hear words and other sounds with our ears. Some animal noises sound like words!

## Who's Who?

"Whooo! Whooo!" says the owl.

**Say the word for each picture. Circle the pictures that have the same oo sound as in whooo.**

## A Sweet Tweet

"Tweet! Tweet!" says the bird.

**Say the word for each picture. Circle the pictures that have the same long e sound as in tweet.**

# And Now, Meow

"Meow!" says the cat.

**Say the word for each picture. Circle the pictures that have the same ow sound as in meow.**

# Make Some Noise

Animals make noises to talk to each other and to scare away other animals. Can you hear any animal sounds right now?

**EARLY CONCEPTS**

## Quiet or Not Quiet?

Can you tell which of these animals are making some noise? Circle the next picture in each pattern.

A lion's roar can be heard five miles (8 km) away!

# Noisy Animals

Some animals are louder than others.

**Circle the pictures that show animals making noise.**

# Cover Your Ears!

A whisper is a quiet noise. A scream is a loud noise! Animals can be quiet or loud. What loud animals can you think of?

**MATH**

## Big and Loud

This animal is the largest on Earth. It can whistle loudly. Its call is as loud as a jet plane! What is it?

**Connect the dots in the right order from 1 to 25 to find out.**

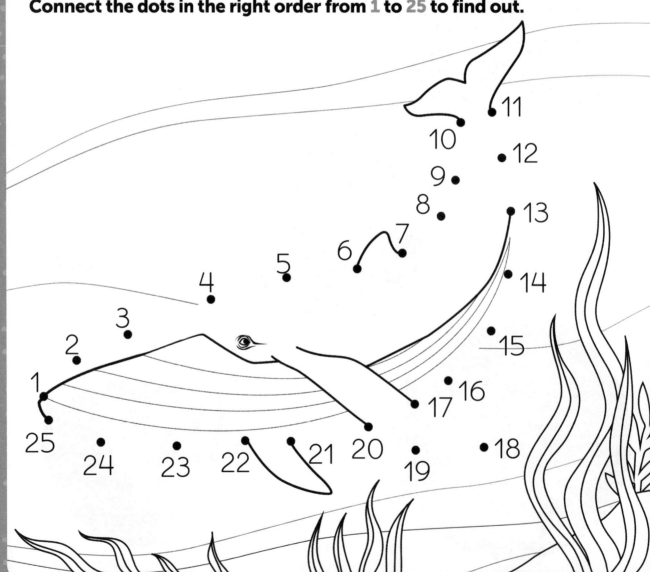

# Code Breaker

**Code**

1 = a    2 = b    3 = e    4 = h

5 = l    6 = u    7 = w

Name one of the loudest animals on Earth!

**Use the code above to figure out what letter goes with each number.**

**Fill in the correct letters to spell out the animal's name.**

2    5    6    3

7    4    1    5    3

# Which Is Loudest?

**?** What is the loudest animal you have ever heard?

**Circle the animal you think makes the loudest noise.**

117

# Touchy Feely

How can you tell if something feels hard or soft? Touch it!
We can touch things with our hands to learn more about them.

## Feeling Your Way

Follow the maze in two ways. First, find the path from the hand to the word soft. Second, find the path from the hand to the word hard.

soft                                    hard

# Soft or Hard?

**Can you tell which of these things are soft and which things are hard?**
**Circle the word that best describes the picture.**

soft     hard

soft     hard

soft     hard

soft     hard

soft     hard

soft     hard

# A Sense of Things

When you touch something, you can tell if it feels warm or cool.
Your hands are very good at feeling hot and cold.

**EARLY CONCEPTS**

## Hot or Cold?

**Help get the cold things into the freezer!**
**Circle the things that are cold.**

120

# What's It Like Outside?

Some places are hot. Others are cold.

**Write an H next to the places that are hot. Write a C next to the places that are cold.**

# The Nose Knows

You can use your nose to smell. Animals use their noses, too. Animals use their sense of smell to find food and to stay safe.

## I Know a Rhyme

Words rhyme when they have the same ending sound, like nose and rose.

**Say the word for each picture. Circle the pictures that rhyme with nose and rose.**

# I Need a Nose!

**Oh no! Where are the animals' noses? Draw a nose on each animal.**

# How Does That Smell?

Your nose gives you information about the world around you. Fruit smells good until it gets old. Then it's stinky!

**EARLY CONCEPTS**

## Smelly Sorting

Circle the things that smell good. Cross out the things that smell bad.

A skunk uses its smelly spray to chase away predators.

**Q** What did one eye say to the other eye?

# R as in Rose!

This rose smells sweet! The word rose begins with r.

**Circle the animals whose names start with the same sound as the r in rose.**

**A** "Something between us smells!"

125

# So Tasty!

Taste is one of the five senses. We use our tongues to taste food. What foods are your favorites?

**EARLY CONCEPTS**

## What's for Lunch?

These animals are hungry.

**Draw a line from each animal to its favorite food.**

# A Taste of the Garden

This garden grows all kinds of foods!

**Count the number of each kind of food you see. Then write each number in the chart below.**

The flavor of a food comes from the senses of taste and smell working together.

**Foods Grown in the Garden**

| pumpkin | lettuce | corn | carrot | tomato |
|---------|---------|------|--------|--------|
|         |         |      |        |        |

# Touch and Go

Some animals use their whiskers to feel. Insects use their antennae to feel.

whiskers

antennae

## Wonderful Whiskers

**Circle the animals that have whiskers.**

# Awesome Antennae

Circle the animals that have antennae.

Whiskers help animals notice changes in the air. This can help them find their way in the dark.

# How Do You Feel?

What does this bear use to touch and feel things around it? Connect the dots in the right order from **A** to **L** to find out.

# See You Later!

Now you know how we use our senses to understand the world around us. You have also learned about how some animals use their senses!

**EARLY CONCEPTS**

## Picture It!

**Now it's your turn. Think of some of the things you can sense around you.**

**Draw something you touch.**

**Draw something you see.**

**Draw something you hear.**

**Draw something you smell.**

**Draw something you taste.**

# CHAPTER 6

In this chapter, we use the word "bug" to include bugs and insects of all kinds.

# Bugs and Friends

**Bugs are on the go all around the planet.** Some crawl. Some fly. Some hop! In this chapter, you'll learn about what makes each creature special. Spot some favorite bug facts as you read.

For every human on Earth, there are more than one billion insects. That's a lot of bugs!

# Ants Are Insects

Ants live all over the world. They live in very large groups called colonies. When was the last time you saw an ant?

## All About A

Ant begins with the letter A.

**Say the word for each picture. Draw a line from the A to the words that start with the same sound as ant.**

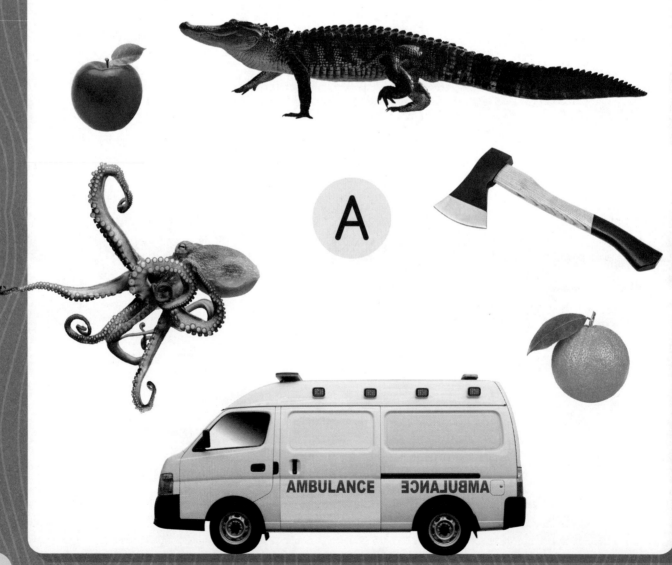

A

AMBULANCE

# 6 Legs

**Did you know that all insects have 6 legs?**
**Circle the insects. Look for 6 legs!**

Ants don't have ears. They "listen" by feeling vibrations through their feet.

red ant

butterfly

dung beetle

centipede

lizard

fly

spider

snail

# Buzzing Bees

Bees buzz as they fly between flowers. They drink nectar. Nectar is a sweet liquid in a flower. Bees also use nectar to make honey.

**LETTERS**

## Busy Bee

**Where did this bee land? Connect the dots in the right order from A to Z to find out.**

Honeybees flap their wings 200 times every second.

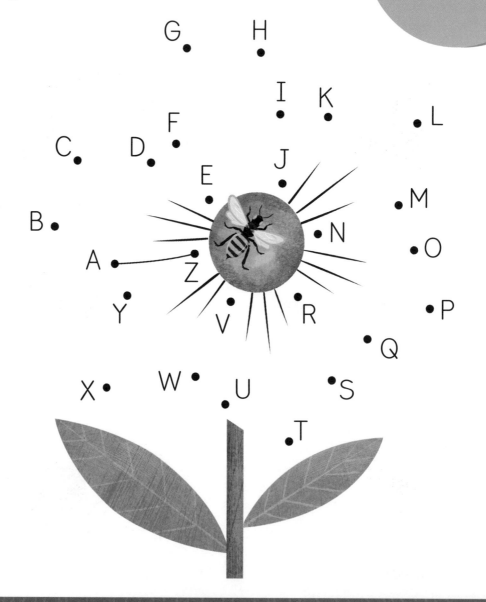

# Flower Power

Bees love flowers.

**Trace the words on the flower.**

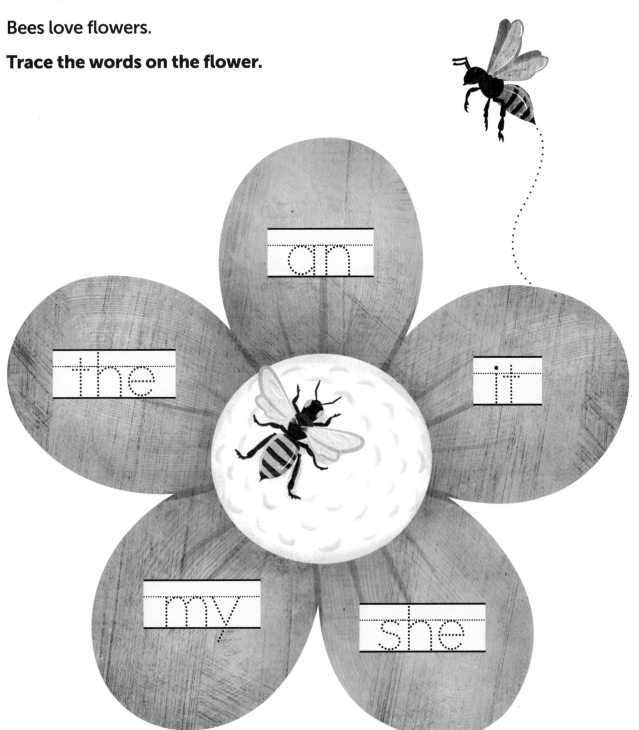

# Beetlemania!

There are around 400,000 kinds of beetles! They are found all over the world. Beetles come in all shapes and sizes.

**EARLY CONCEPTS**

## Beetles Big and Small

**Circle the beetle that is the longest. Draw a square around the beetle that is the shortest.**

dung beetle      Hercules beetle      carrion beetle

**Circle the beetle that is the biggest. Draw a square around the beetle that is the smallest.**

stag beetle      weevil      June bug

# Find Your Way, Beetle!

Bark beetles live in trees. They make trails through the bark.

**Help this beetle find its way out of the tree.**

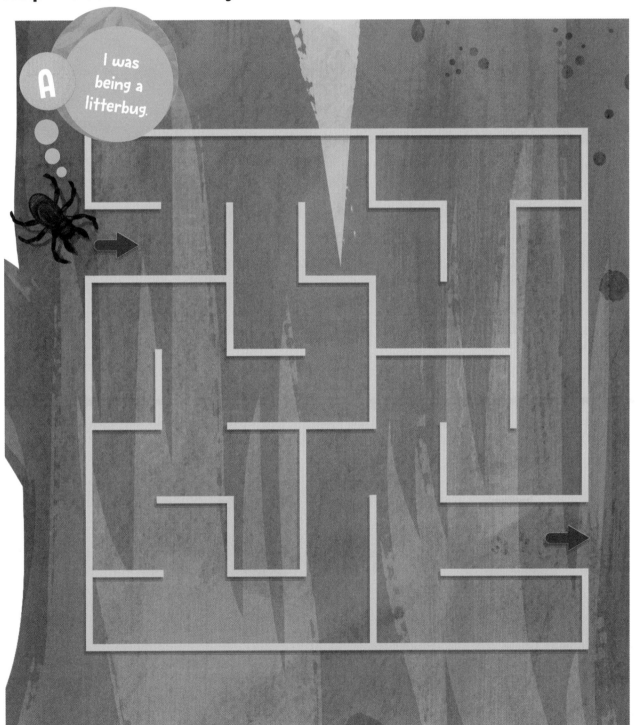

A I was being a litterbug.

# Lovely Ladies

Ladybugs are a kind of beetle. Their bright marks tell predators: "Don't eat me. I taste bad!"

**MATH**  **WRITING**

## Spot It

Count the spots on each ladybug. Write the number below each one. Then write the number of spots for each pair of ladybugs.

  +

_____  +  _____  =  _____

  +

_____  +  _____  =  _____

# Snug as a Bug

Say the word for each picture. Circle the words that rhyme with **bug**.

# Which Lady Comes Next?

Circle the ladybug that completes the pattern.

# Becoming a Butterfly

A butterfly changes a lot before it becomes an adult! First, a caterpillar hatches from an egg. Then, the caterpillar eats and grows. Next, the caterpillar builds a soft, thin shell around itself. This is called a pupa. Finally, a butterfly comes out of the pupa.

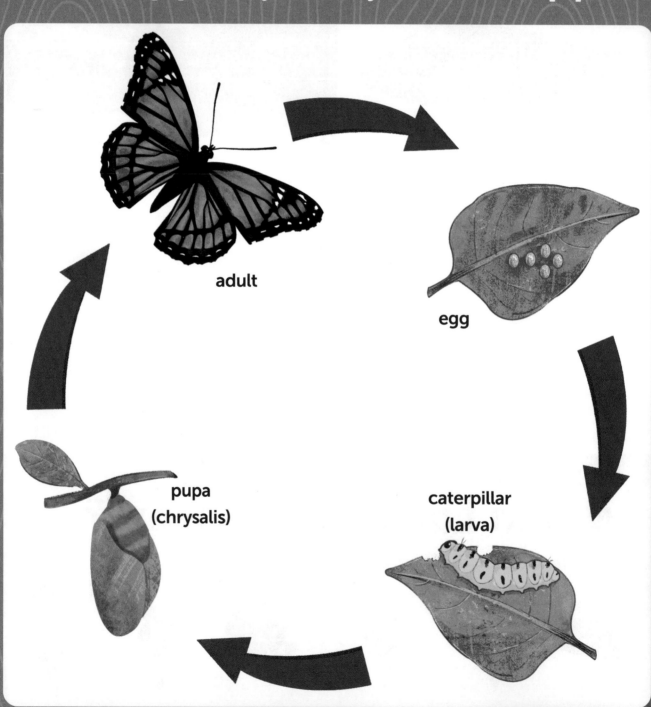

adult

egg

caterpillar
(larva)

pupa
(chrysalis)

# Get It in Order

Write a number on each line to show the order of the steps in a butterfly's life cycle. The first number has been written for you.

# Inch by Inch

An inchworm is a tiny caterpillar. Inchworms eat leaves, branches, and the bark of trees. An inchworm will grow to become a moth.

**MATH**

## Inching Along

An inchworm is about 1 inch (2.5 cm) long. You can use an inchworm to measure.

**Circle the object that is the same length as the inchworm.**

---

**Circle the object that is 3 inchworms long.**

**?** What other things are about as long as an inchworm?

# Marigold Code

**Use the code to color the picture.**

Code

**g** = green      **o** = orange

**r** = red      **y** = yellow

145

# Spot the Spiders

Have you ever seen a spider? These crawly creatures have 8 legs. Many spiders spin webs to catch a tasty meal.

## Give Me Legs!

Draw **8** legs on the spider.

The world's largest spider is the goliath bird-eating spider.

## Who's Next?

Circle the spider that comes next in the pattern.

146

# Look-Alike Webs

Can you find two webs that are the same? Circle them.

# Buggy Match

The world is filled with all kinds of bugs. They can be different colors, shapes, and sizes. What bugs have you seen where you live?

**EARLY CONCEPTS**

## Color Me Beautiful

Bugs come in many different colors.

**Draw a line to match each bug with its color.**

**giraffe weevil**

blue

**butterfly**

red

**mint beetle**

green

**praying mantis**
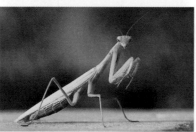
yellow

**EARLY CONCEPTS**

# Fliers and Crawlers

Some of these bugs have wings, but others do not.

**Circle the bugs with wings.**

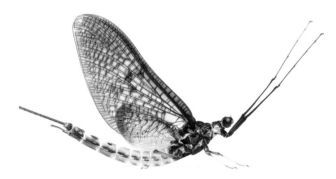

# Flap Those Wings!

Dragonflies have long, thin bodies. Many have wings that you can see through. These fast fliers live near ponds, lakes, and streams.

**EARLY CONCEPTS**  **READING**  **WRITING**

## Write It, Picture It

**Trace the words in the sentence. Then draw a picture to match the sentence.**

A big dragonfly  leaf.

# D as in Dragonfly

Dragonfly begins with the letter D.

**Say the word for each picture. Draw a line from the D to the words that start with the same sound as dragonfly.**

Dragonflies have large, round eyes that allow them to see in all directions.

D

# Light It Up!

Q Why do spiders eat fireflies?

Have you ever seen fireflies on a summer night? These beautiful beetles light up! The flashing patterns send messages.

A For a light snack.

**READING**

## Fly Away Rhyme

Firefly **ends with the word** fly.

**Circle the things that rhyme with** fly.

# So Many Fireflies

**Write the number of fireflies in each group on the lines below.**
**Add them together to get the total.**

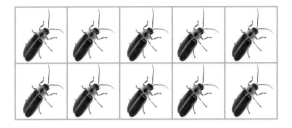 +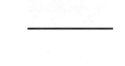

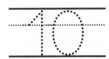 + _____ = _____

---

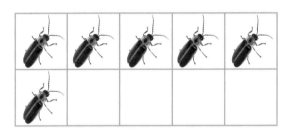 +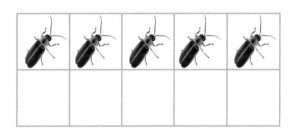

_____ + _____ = _____

---

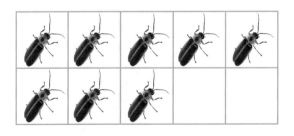 +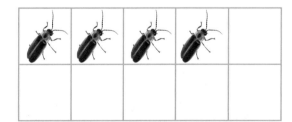

_____ + _____ = _____

# A Hop and a Song

*Boing!* Grasshoppers use their strong back legs to jump far.
They also chirp by rubbing their back legs against their wings.

## Champion Jumper

**Which grasshopper jumped the farthest? Circle it.**

# Alphabet Hop

Help the grasshopper learn the alphabet. Write the letters in order as it hops from leaf to leaf.

**?** Grasshoppers have three small eyes and two large eyes. How many eyes do they have all together?

# Bug Science

Some people study insects! These scientists learn where insects live. They learn what they eat. They learn how they grow.

**EARLY CONCEPTS** | **MATH** | **WRITING**

## Crawly Collections

A scientist wants to fill a box with 6 different insects.

**How many more does she need? Draw the insects in the empty boxes to make 6 in all.**

The scientist needs _____ more insects.

**?** What would you like to learn about insects?

# Syllable Counting

The word bug has just 1 word part, or syllable. Say the name of each bug aloud. Circle the bugs that have 1 syllable.

bee

moth

beetle

ant

cricket

The word grasshopper has 3 syllables. Say each word aloud. Circle the words with 3 syllables.

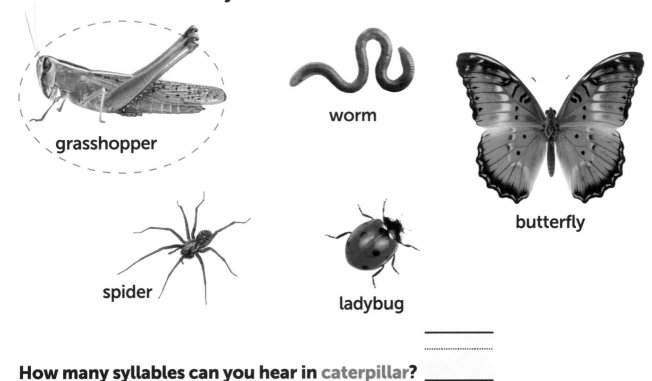

grasshopper

worm

butterfly

spider

ladybug

How many syllables can you hear in caterpillar? _____

# Bye-Bye, Bugs!

Show what you know about our creepy-crawly friends. Name three things you learned about bugs. What do you still want to know more about?

**EARLY CONCEPTS**

## My Butterfly Pal

**Make the butterfly beautiful. Color it with your favorite colors.**

# Find Those Bugs

Look at the names of the bugs in the box. Circle each name in the word search. Look across and down.

**ant    spider    moth    fly    bee    worm**

| A | N | T | B | X | S |
|---|---|---|---|---|---|
| W | C | O | E | G | P |
| O | M | K | E | S | I |
| R | F | L | Y | H | D |
| M | O | T | H | U | E |
| G | H | Z | J | Q | R |

# CHAPTER 7

Baby polar bears are called cubs. They weigh about as much as a loaf of bread when they are born.

# Baby Animals

**Play with a puppy and swim with ducklings!** In this chapter, you'll get to know the cutest baby animals on land, in the air, and under the water. Can you find your favorites?

# Babies on the Move

Many baby animals can walk, swim, or crawl pretty soon after they are born. They may be a bit wobbly at first, though!

**EARLY CONCEPTS**

## Find My Mom

Uh-oh, these babies got lost! Match each baby animal to its mom.

162

**?** What baby animals have you seen where you live?

# Is Baby In or On?

**Write in or on to complete the sentence.**

The puppy is ____ its house.

The kitten is ____ the pillow.

The fish are ____ the tank.

The penguin is ____ the snow.

# Let's Play

**Q** What did the teddy bear say after eating? →

Do you like to play? So do baby bears! Bear cubs learn how to defend themselves by play fighting.

**MATH** | **WRITING**

## Playful Cubs

How many bear cubs do you see?

**Count them. Then write the number on the line.**

**MATH** | **WRITING**

## So Many Prints

The bear cubs left behind many paw prints after their game.

**Count the paw prints. Write the number on the line.**

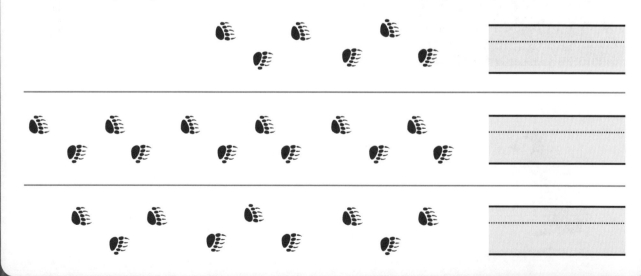

A

I'm stuffed!

# Playtime Favorites

Just like bear cubs, kids love to play, too!
Here are some favorite toys and games.

**Write the missing letter in each word.**

t___p

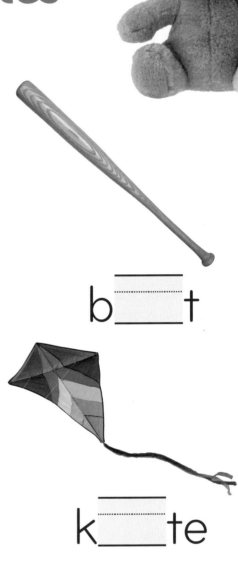

b___t

n___t

k___te

g___mes

c___be

# Little Foxes, Big Ears

The fennec fox is a small fox with big ears! When these cubs grow up, they will use their big ears to listen for prey.

**MATH** | **WRITING**

## How Many Ears?

**Count the ears on both foxes.**

The foxes' big ears also help keep them cool.

The foxes have  ears.

# Listen for the Fox

Circle the things that rhyme with **fox**.

# Seals by the Sea

Baby seals are called pups. They drink their mother's milk for a few weeks. Then they begin to hunt on their own for fish to eat.

**MATH** | **WRITING**

## Dinnertime!

This baby seal is hungry!

**Count the fish below before the pup eats them.**

**Write the number on the line.**

# A Real Meal for a Seal

Real and meal rhyme with seal.

**Circle the picture whose name rhymes with seal.**

**MATH** **WRITING**

# Counting Steps

This number trail leads to the baby seals. But the rain washed away some of the numbers!

**Can you write in the missing numbers?**

# Bamboo Babies

Would you want to eat the same thing every day? Giant pandas do! They eat almost nothing but bamboo.

**EARLY CONCEPTS** | **MATH** | **WRITING**

## More Bamboo?

This baby panda wants 10 stalks of bamboo to eat.

**Count the stalks.**

**How many are there? Write the answer on the line.** _____

**Are there enough? Circle the answer.**     Yes          No

**Draw more stalks of bamboo so there are 10 in all.**

**How many bamboo stalks did you draw?**

_____

**Write the answer on the line.** _____

# A Changing Cub

A baby panda is called a cub.

**Read the word** cub.

**Change the b to p. Write the new word below.**

**Read the new word.**

**Now change the c to p. Write the new word below.**

A panda weighs about the same as a pencil when it is born!

**Draw a picture of the last new word.**

# Hungry Raccoons

Pandas are picky, but some animals are not. Raccoons eat almost anything! They even eat trash out of garbage cans.

**MATH** | **READING**

## Clap and Count

Which foods do you think baby raccoons would like?

**Say the name of each food out loud. Clap once for each word part, or syllable. Circle how many syllables you hear.**

1　　2　　3　　　　1　　2　　3　　　　1　　2　　3

1　　2　　3　　　　1　　2　　3　　　　1　　2　　3

# Runaway Word

The word the has run away!

**Write the to complete each sentence.**

I see _____ raccoon.

Do you see _____ raccoon?

What does _____ raccoon eat?

# My Favorite Food

Raccoons aren't picky, but they have some favorites. So do you!

**Draw a picture of your favorite food.**




**Say the name of your favorite food. How many syllables does it have?**

_____

**Write the number on the line.** _____

# Big Change Babies

Some baby animals go through big changes as they grow, like a caterpillar becoming a butterfly!

## All Grown Up

**Draw a line to show what each baby will look like when it grows up.**

caterpillar

frog

larva

monarch butterfly

tadpole

ladybug

# How Many Are Left?

There were **7** butterflies, then **2** flew away.

**How many are left?**

Write the answer on the line. _____

There were **3** ladybugs, then **1** flew away.

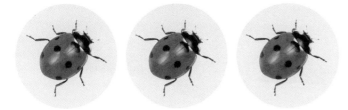

**How many are left?**

Write the answer on the line. _____

There were **10** frogs, then **8** hopped away.

**How many are left?**

Write the answer on the line. _____

# Pint-Size Pets

**Q** What did the cat say after it told a joke? ↓

Puppies, kittens, bunnies, and other baby pets like to play. What are some ways these baby pets can play?

**MATH**

## Who Has More?

**Circle the puppy with more bones.**

**Circle the kitten with more balls of yarn.**

# Funny Bunny Math

Oh no! These bunnies got into the number cards.

**Circle the bunny holding the higher number.**

# Quack!

Baby ducks are called ducklings. They can swim when they are just one week old.

**MATH** | **READING** | **WRITING**

## Rhyming Riddle

Count the ducklings.
How many do you see?
If one gets lost, how
many will there be?

Can you answer the riddle?

There will be _____ ducklings.

The words see and be rhyme.

**Circle see and be in the riddle.**

**Now circle pictures of things that rhyme with see and be.**

# Picture Riddle

**How many V's can you find in this picture? Circle them.**

**? Ducks and other birds fly together in a V-shape. Can you see the V?**

# On the Savanna

Many kinds of baby animals live on the plains of Africa. These grassy plains are often called savannas.

## Z as in Zebra

The word zebra begins with z. Say the word for each picture.

**Circle the things that begin with the z sound, like zebra.**

## E as in Elephant

Elephant begins with a short e sound. Say the word for each picture.

**Circle the thing that begins with the short e sound, like elephant.**

# Tall, Taller, Tallest

Giraffes have long legs and long necks. They are so tall!

**Circle the giraffe that is the tallest. Draw a line under the giraffe that is the shortest.**

All zebras have stripes, but no two zebras have the same pattern.

# Bye-Bye, Babies

You have met some amazing baby animals. You met cubs and pups. You met chicks and kittens. Now it's time to say goodbye!

**EARLY CONCEPTS** **WRITING**

## My Favorite Baby

**Draw a picture of your favorite baby animal.**

**Write the name of the animal.**

# Baby Me

**Draw a picture of you when you were a baby.**

**Write your name.**

# CHAPTER 8

# Dino Days

**Dinosaurs and other prehistoric creatures lived many millions of years ago.** They roamed Earth long before humans existed. In this chapter, you'll meet some of these amazing creatures that once called Earth home.

**Did you know?** Not all dinosaurs were gray or brown. Many dinosaurs were bright colors!

# A World of Dinos

Dinosaurs could be huge or tiny. Some could swim, and some could fly. Scientists have found the bones of hundreds of different kinds of dinosaurs!

BRONTOSAURUS

GUEMESIA

# Get to Know Them

Here are some dinosaurs that once lived on Earth.

**Trace the first letter of each name.**

Not all dinosaurs lived on Earth at the same time.

Triceratops

Velociraptor

Stegosaurus

Iguanodon

# Filling the Sky

Imagine seeing a flying dinosaur! Real flying dinos had long wings. Some dinosaurs had feathers, like birds today.

**MATH**

## Dino Dots

*Microraptor* knew how to fly.

**Connect the dots in the right order from 1 to 20 to see what it looked like.**

# High Fliers

**Circle the dinosaur holding the highest number.**

# T. Rex Time

*Tyrannosaurus rex* is called *T. rex* for short. This giant meat-eater was as heavy as the biggest African elephants today!

**LETTERS** **READING** **WRITING**

## A Dino Beginning

*T. rex* begins with the letter T. Trace the letters.

**Place a check mark next to the pictures of things that begin with the t sound.**

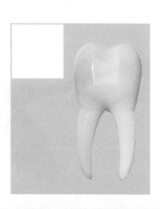

# A Dino Ending

*T. rex* had the largest teeth of any dinosaur!

*T. rex* ends with the letter x.

**Place a check mark next to the pictures of things that end with the x sound.**

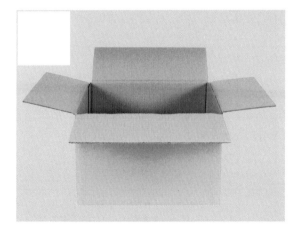

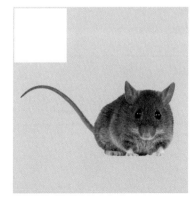

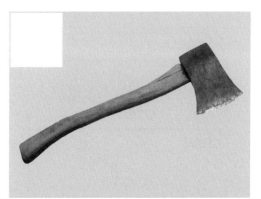

# From Head to Tail

*Brontosaurus* was a giant plant-eater with a long neck and small head. Its tail alone was 50 feet (15 m) long!

## Hidden Dino Words

Dinosaurs had lots of different body parts.

**Circle the names of the dino body parts pictured below the word search. Look across and down.**

*Brontosaurus* means "thunder lizard."

| P | T | O | O | T | H | S |
|---|---|---|---|---|---|---|
| G | B | H | K | E | G | C |
| H | O | R | N | P | N | A |
| A | N | L | E | G | I | L |
| C | E | C | L | A | W | E |

| bone 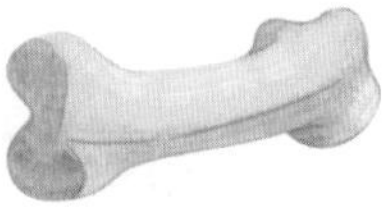 | horn 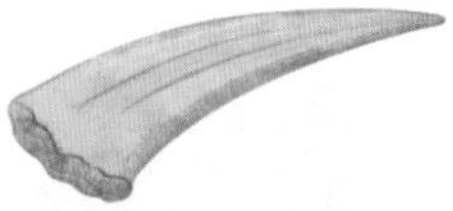 | scale 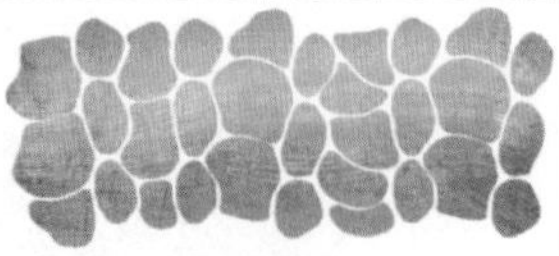 |
|---|---|---|
| claw  | leg  | tooth  |

192

# Parts and Pieces

**Label the parts of the *Brontosaurus*.**
**Use the words in the blue box.**

| eye | mouth | tail |
|-----|-------|------|
| neck | leg | back |

? How are you like a dinosaur?
How are you different?

_____ _____ eye

_____ _____ _____

# Prehistoric Pals

Many dinosaurs traveled in groups called herds or packs.
This kept them safe from predators.

## Find My Kind

These dinosaurs can't find their friends!

**Draw a line to pair each dinosaur with one of the same kind.**

# Staying Together

*T. rex* hunted in packs.

**Use the color code to color the picture.**

Code

**can = brown**
**has = green**
**we  = pink**

**Trace each word from the color code. Then write it on the line.**

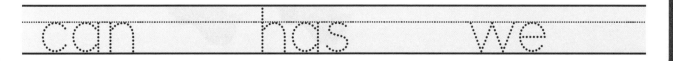

can          has          we

# Triceratops Is Tops

*Triceratops* is famous for its horns and spiky head plates. It looked fierce! But it ate only plants.

**MATH**  **WRITING**

## Addition Party

The *Triceratops* dinos are forming groups.

**How large will each group be? Add up the small groups to find the total number of dinosaurs.**

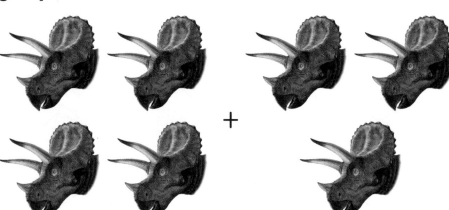

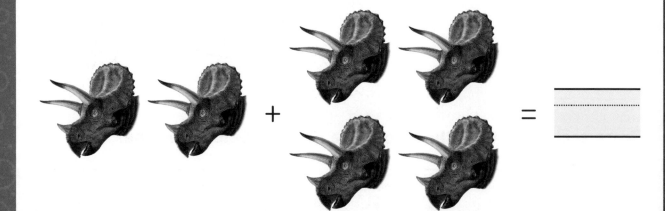

# Snack Time

**Cross out the number of leaves the *Triceratops* dinos ate. How many are left in each group? Write the number on each line.**

The dinosaurs ate 4 leaves.

There are _____ leaves left.

The dinosaurs ate 6 leaves.

There are _____ leaves left.

# From Egg to Dino

A dinosaur started life as an egg. Dinosaur parents kept their eggs safe. What animals today hatch from eggs?

**READING**

## Listen for the E

**Listen for the sound in the middle of each word. Which ones have the same e sound as egg and nest? Circle them.**

**READING**

## Colorful Sounds

**Which color names have an e sound like the one in egg? Circle them.**

# Race to the Nest

Help the mommy dinosaur find her eggs.

**Follow the path from the dinosaur to the eggs.**

FOSSIL OF DINOSAUR EGGS

# Dino Extremes

Dinosaurs came in many shapes and sizes. The biggest was *Titanosaurus*. Tiny *Oculudentavis* weighed less than a pencil!

**MATH** | **WRITING**

## Number Sizes

TITANOSAURUS

The dinosaurs are holding signs with numbers listed in order from lowest to highest.

**Fill in the missing numbers.**

# Record Breaker

This dinosaur holds the record for the longest neck. It was 50 feet (15 m) long! That's longer than a school bus!

**Connect the dots in order from A to Z to see what this dino looked like.**

This dinosaur's scientific name is *Mamenchisaurus sinocanadorum*.

# Stegosaurus Strong

*Stegosaurus* had large bony back plates and long tail spikes.
But this plant-eating dino had a brain the size of a lime!

**READING**

## Starting Sounds

*Stegosaurus* starts with the letters S and t.

**Say the sound: st. What else starts with st? Circle the pictures.**

# Trace the Plates

This *Stegosaurus* has words on its plates.

**Trace the words you see.**

# Dig It!

How do we know about dinosaurs? Scientists dig up their fossils!
Fossils are traces of living things preserved in rock.

**MATH** | **WRITING**

It takes about
**10,000 years**
for a fossil to
form.

# Fossil Count

**How many of each type of fossil are there? How
many are there in all? Write the numbers on the lines.**

 leg bones _____    teeth _____

 skulls _____   total _____

204

# Dino Eggs

Dinosaur eggs are fossils, too. These eggs are in groups of 10.

**Count by 10 to 100. How many rows of eggs are there?**

There are _____ groups of 10.

# Puzzle Pieces

Scientists study fossils to figure out which dino they came from.
Putting together fossils can be like putting together a puzzle!

## Fossil Matchup

**Match each fossil to the dinosaur it may have come from.**

# Grouping Game

These fossils were found in groups. They may have belonged to the same dinosaur.

**Draw circles around the fossil groups.**
**How many groups of 4 are there? Circle them.**

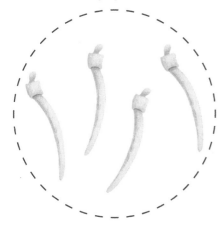
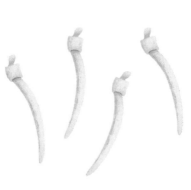
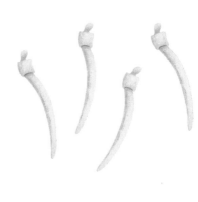

**How many groups of 3 are there? Circle them.**

**How many groups of 2 are there? Circle them.**

# Read About Dinos

You can learn a lot about dinosaurs from books!
Do you have a favorite book about dinosaurs?

**READING**

## Check It Out

The title of a book tells what it is about. The author is the person who wrote the book. The illustrator is the person who drew the pictures.

**Look at the book. Circle the title. Underline the author's name.**

ALL ABOUT DINOS
by Shruti Aggarwal

Illustrations by Kailien Singson

# Your Turn

**Draw the cover of a book you would like to make.**

**Write the title. Write your name as the author or illustrator.**

? Would you rather be an author or an illustrator or both? Why?

# Back From the Past

You learned about some dinosaurs that roamed Earth long ago. You found out what makes each one special. You learned how scientists know about them. What else do you want to know about dinosaurs?

**EARLY CONCEPTS**

## Dino Favorites

Draw the dinosaur you liked learning about most. Color your dinosaur. Then write its name below it.

# Dino-Mazing

Follow the path of the maze that spells the word **DINO**.
Say each letter's sound as you go.

# CHAPTER 9

# On the Move

**Beep, beep!** Cars, trucks, trains, planes, boats, bikes—they are all on the move every day. In this chapter, you will learn about things that go, go, go! What is your favorite way to travel?

Some super-speedy trains in Japan can travel up to 200 miles an hour (320 km/h)!

# Things That Go

**Q** Why can't a bike stand on its own?

The world is filled with all kinds of things that go! These are forms of transportation. They move people and things around.

**READING** **WRITING**

## Transportation Scramble

These words are all names of different kinds of transportation.

**Unscramble each word. Write each word on the line. Look at the pictures to help you.**

**A**

It's two-tired!

ekib _____

ubs _____

rca _____

obta _____

# Where Does It Go?

Match the vehicle with the place where it moves. Draw a line to connect the pictures that go together.

# Let's Go!

Vacations can be a lot of fun! Part of the fun is getting there. Have you ever been on a vacation? How did you travel there?

**WRITING**

## Puzzles That Go

**Write the words that match the pictures in the crossword puzzle. Some words you will write down. Some words you will write across.**

### Down

1.

3.

5.

### Across

2.

4.

**EARLY CONCEPTS**

# What Moves?

Can you think of another way people might get from place to place? Draw a picture of something else that moves.

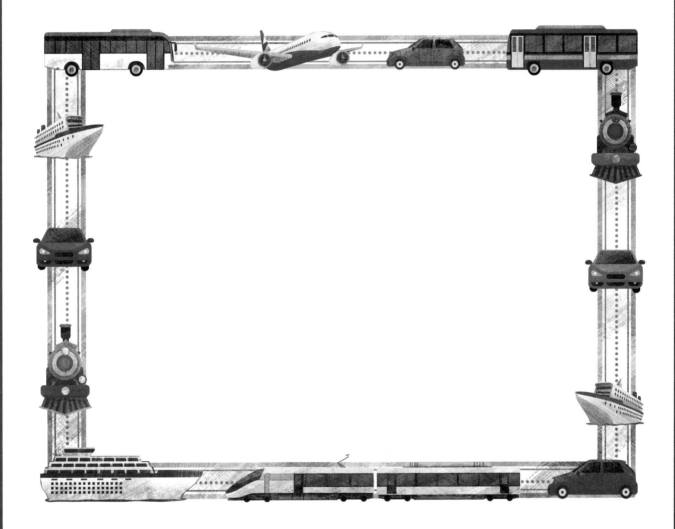

**READING**  **WRITING**

# You Are on the Go!

Trace the word in the sentence.

We can 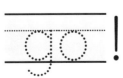 !

# Wonderful Wheels

Wheels help us move things quickly and easily.
What things do you know of that use wheels?

## The Shape of a Wheel

**What is the same shape as a wheel? Circle your answer.**

Skateboard wheels used to be made out of clay.

# A Parade of Wheels

Wheels are everywhere!

Count the number of wheels on each vehicle. How many do you see in all? Write the number on the line.

# There are _____ wheels.

# Moving Sounds

*Vroom! Honk!* These are the sounds of a car.
What sounds do other vehicles make?

**READING**

## Vehicle Rhymes

**Circle the rhyming words in each sentence.**

### 1. The boat must float.

### 2. The car can go far.

### 3. That truck is stuck!

### 4. Come with us on the bus.

# Vehicle Names

**Say the words in each row. If they start with the same sound, circle the words. If they do not, cross them out.**

train

truck

plane

bike

bus

boat

**Which two vehicle words rhyme? Write each word on a line below.**

_____      _____

# Traffic Tie-Ups

Traffic jams happen when there are too many vehicles on the road at one time. Some places have more traffic jams than others.

**MATH** | **WRITING**

## Traffic Tally

There's a traffic jam in the city.

**Count the buses, trucks, and cars.**
**Write the number of each on the lines.**

_____ buses    _____ trucks    _____ cars

# Out of a Jam

**Help the big car get to the city. Draw a path from the car to the city.**

? Have you ever been in a traffic jam? What did you do?

# On the Job

Some vehicles have work to do. Think about some vehicles you know of that do work. What are the vehicles on this page doing?

## Vehicle Opposites

These vehicles are different, but they all have work to do.

**Draw a line to match each word to its opposite.**

big

under

fast

small

over

slow

# Work to Do

**Trace the name of each vehicle below its picture.**

Firefighting planes help put out fires in areas that fire trucks cannot reach easily.

tractor

tugboat

fire truck

# Take a Bike Ride

Bicycles are a fun way to get from one place to another.
Do you ride a bike? Where do you like to ride it?

**EARLY CONCEPTS**  **MATH**

## To the Ice-Cream Shop!

Help the bike riders follow the pattern to get to the ice-cream shop.

**Fill in the pattern with the next correct shape.**

# The Wheels on the Bikes

**How many wheels are on all the red bikes? How many wheels are on all the blue bikes? Write the numbers on the lines.**

_____ wheels on red bikes

_____ wheels on blue bikes

**How many wheels in total? Write a number sentence.**

_____ + _____ = _____

The city of Amsterdam has more bikes than cars.

# All Aboard!

Trains have been around for over 200 years. That's longer than there have been automobiles!

**MATH**  **WRITING**

## On the Tracks

Freight trains can have many cars!

**Help count some of the train cars by filling in the missing numbers in order.**

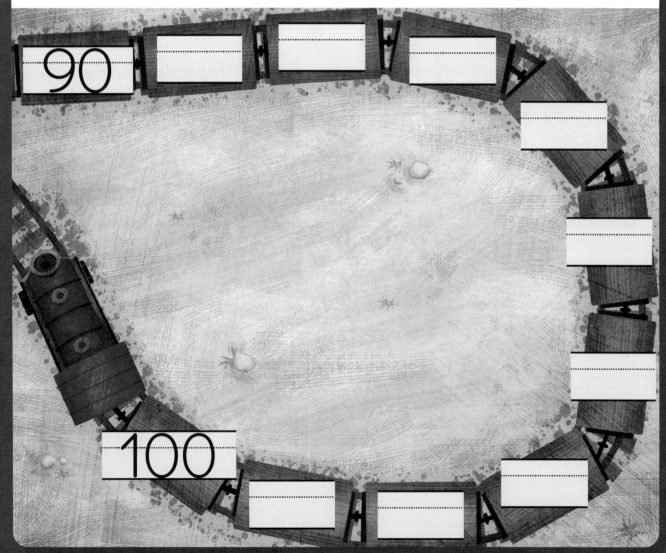

90

100

# Out of Sight

**Trace the words on the train cars. Read them aloud. Color the train.**

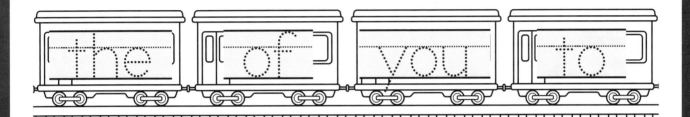

the of you to

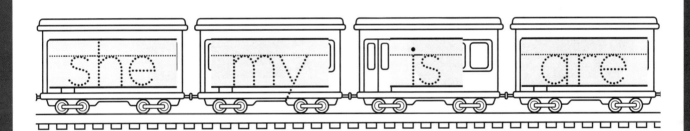

she my is are

do does

# Speed It Up!

Vehicles go different speeds. Some vehicles go fast, like airplanes. Others go slower, like bikes.

## Fast Cars

We measure speeds by saying how far a vehicle can go in an hour.

**Which car is going the fastest? Circle the picture.**

65 miles per hour

34 miles per hour

53 miles per hour

71 miles per hour

# Faster or Slower?

Some vehicles move faster than others.

**Circle the picture that answers each question.**

**Which one will go faster?**

**Which one will go slower?**

**Which one will go faster?**

# Trucks on the Move

Different kinds of trucks are used for different things. They look different, too. Have you ever seen trucks like the ones below?

## Working Trucks

Draw a line from each truck to the work it can help with.

# Rock Pickup

The truck can only carry 4 rocks at a time!

**Circle groups of 4 rocks. How many groups are there?**
**Write the number on the line.**

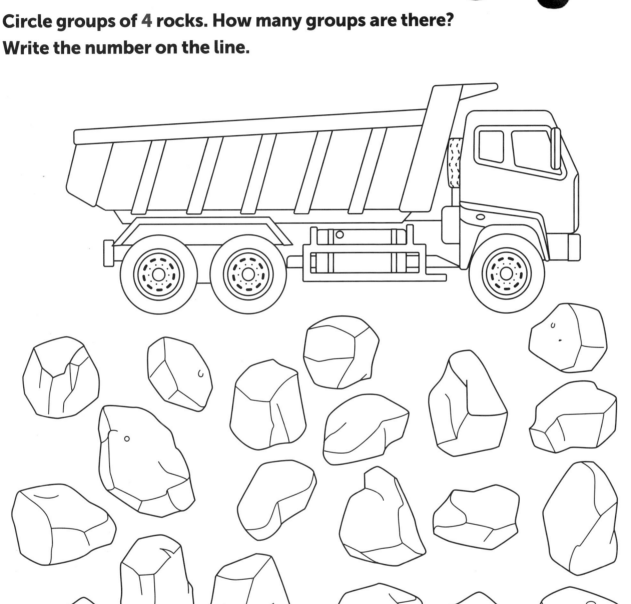

_____ groups

# To the Rescue!

Some vehicles are extra special because they are used to help others. These cars and trucks are useful in emergencies.

**LETTERS** **READING**

## F as in Fire Truck

Time to put out the fire!

**Circle the pictures that show things that start with the same sound as fire truck.**

# Who's the Helper?

Connect the dots in the right order from 80 to 100.
What vehicle did you draw? Color the vehicle.

Not all fire trucks are red. They can be yellow, green, or white!

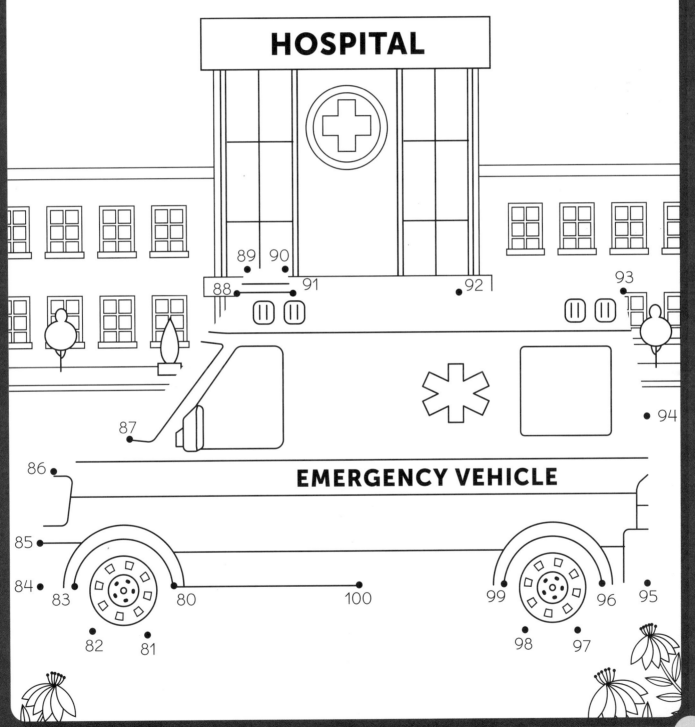

HOSPITAL

EMERGENCY VEHICLE

# In the Sky

Some vehicles travel through the sky, like planes and helicopters. Hot-air balloons are a fun way to see the world around you!

## Pretty Balloons

**Join the hot-air balloon festival! Look at the patterns on the balloons. Circle the balloon that comes next in each row.**

# Where to Next?

The plane must make **11** stops. Connect the dots
in the right order from **1** to **11** to make them.
What shape did the plane make?

Hot-air
balloons are
another way
to travel
up high!

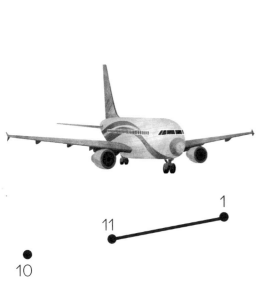

2

1

11

10

3

4

9

5

7

8

6

# Time to Go!

You learned all about things that go. Now it's time to answer the question from the beginning of the chapter: What is your favorite way to travel?

**EARLY CONCEPTS**

## That's Me!

**Draw yourself in the vehicle you chose. Where are you going? Write your name on the drawing.**

# Dream Trip

**Where would you like to go on your travels? Draw it in the space below. Why do you want to go there? Write your answer or ask someone to write your words below the drawing.**

# Answer Key

## Chapter 1: Under the Sea

### p. 9

**Find the One**

### pp. 10–11

**Double Bubble**

**Ready to Pop!**

### pp. 12–13

**Pretty Patterns**

**Find the Corals**

### p. 15

**What Starts With D?**

Circle the deer, dog, and duck.

### p. 17

**Wiggly Fives**

Possible responses:

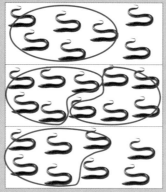

### pp. 18–19

**Fish Find**

**Reef Maze**

### pp. 20–21

**Around the Globe**

**Hidden Turtles**

### pp. 22–23

**Feeding Time!**

**Which One Belongs?**

### p. 24

**Big or Small?**

**p. 27**

**What's Hiding?**

## Chapter 2: In the Rainforest

**pp. 32—33**

**A Fig Feast**
There are 6 figs.

**The Search for Figs**

**p. 35**

**Rainforest Friends**
Draw lines to the leopard and to the ladybug.

**pp. 36—37**

**Where Am I?**

**A Monkey Meal**

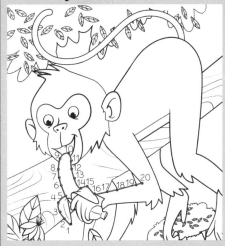

**pp. 38—39**

**Nighttime Rhyme**
Circle the kite and light.

**Day and Night!**
*D* should be next to the top left and bottom right photos. *N* should be next to the top right and bottom left photos.

**In the Night Sky**
Stars and the moon should be circled.

**pp. 40—41**

**It's the Same Sound**
Circle the toes and boat.

**Leaf Math**

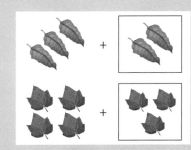

There are a total of 5 leaves in the top row and 7 leaves in the bottom row.

**pp. 42—43**

**Sticking Together**
There are 6 parrots on the branch.

**A Splash of Color!**

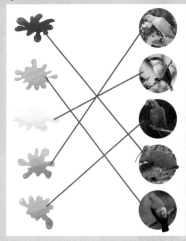

**p. 45**

**Color Me Perfect**

**pp. 46—47**

**Where's the Rain?**
<u>rain</u>forest, <u>rain</u>bow, <u>rain</u>drop

**What Happens Next?**
1: middle photo; 2: bottom photo; 3: top photo

**pp. 48—49**

**What Begins With S?**
Circle the sun, sand, and snake.

**Snake Shapes**

**pp. 50–51**
**Fly, Fly, Fly!**

There are 4 groups of 3.

**Hop to It!**

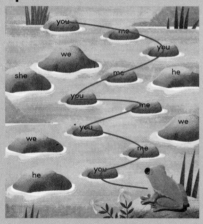

**Chapter 3: Desert Fun**
**pp. 56–57**

**Spot the Animals**

**Stay Cool**

**pp. 58–59**
**Hold That Water**
Circle the cactus on the right.

**Ready for the Journey**
Containers that hold more are:
Row 1: right; Row 2: left;
Row 3: right

**pp. 60–61**
**What Does It Start With?**
Circle the wing and wind.

**Shadow Match**

**p. 63**
**"X" It Out**
Place *X*'s over the octopus, fish, and whale.

**p. 65**
**How Many Leaves?**

The plant had 8 leaves. I drew 2 more leaves to make 10.

**pp. 66–67**
**Catch Some *Z*'s**
Circle the zebra and zipper.

**Home Sweet Home**

**pp. 68–69**
**What's That Creature?**

**Scorpion Shapes**

**pp. 70–71**
**Size Wise**

**Listen to the E**
Circle the words "heat," "meat," "beak," and "seat."

## p. 73
### Do the Math
There are 5 camels, 6 snakes, 6 cactuses, and 9 turtles.

## pp. 74–75
### Plants All Around

### Joshua Tree
Place *X*'s next to "jar" and "juice."

## pp. 76–77
### Tell About It
Circle the words "chilly," "dry," and "icy," and place *X*'s over the words "hot," "sandy," and "rainy."

### Go Home, Penguin!

## p. 78
### What Lives There?
Circle the lizard, snake, and camel.

## Chapter 4: School Days
### pp. 82–83
### Red Shirt, Blue Shirt
There are 5 children with red shirts and 7 children with blue shirts. More children have blue shirts.

### Letter the Way

## p. 85
### B is the Best!
Draw lines from *Bb* to the bus, blocks, book, and beach ball.

## pp. 86–87
### Jump to It!
The missing numbers are 7, 8, 9, 11, 12, and 13.

### Time to Share
There are 5 blocks, 7 teddy bears, 9 tennis balls, and 10 cars.

## pp. 88–89
### Pick a P
Circle the popcorn, pineapple, pretzel, peach, and pear.

### It's a Pizza Pie
There are 8 slices of pizza. There are 6 slices of pizza left after Nan ate 2.

### A Piece of Pizza, Please!
Draw a square around the piece of pizza with 7 circles.

## pp. 90–91
### It's Raining Raisins!
There are 5 raisins on the first piece of celery, 3 on the second, 8 on the third, and 10 on the fourth.

### Reading a Recipe
The steps should be 1. Wash the celery; 2. Spread peanut butter on the celery; 3. Add raisins; and 4. Eat and enjoy!

## pp. 92–93
### Oh! It's an Oboe
Circle the coat, phone, rope, boat, and snowman.

### Sort the Supplies
Draw lines from Mia to the guitar, drum, violin, and xylophone, and from Adam to the paintbrushes, scissors, paint, and canvas.

## pp. 94–95
### Refill the Paint Tray

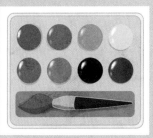

### Paint by Number

## pp. 96–97
### Flat or Solid?
Write an *F* below the first, third, and fourth shapes. Write an *S* below the second, fifth, and sixth shapes.

## Shapes and More Shapes

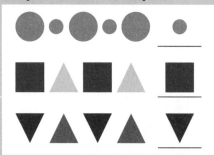

### pp. 98–99
### Scoop It Up

### Find the Party!

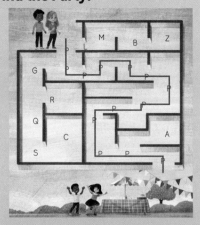

### pp. 100–101
### Ball Count
There are 8 balls.

### Ready to Climb

### pp. 102–103
### Budding Buddies
Circle the flower on the far right.

### Along the Garden Path
The missing letters, in order, are M, N, O, Q, and T.

### p. 105
### School Words

| X | G | E | B | W | P |
|---|---|---|---|---|---|
| S | C | H | O | O | L |
| M | B | W | O | D | A |
| A | R | T | K | G | Y |
| T | Z | C | S | A | E |
| H | B | U | S | R | O |

## Chapter 5: All the Senses
### pp. 108–109
### Bear Sense
Draw a line from "hear" to ears, from "see" to eyes, from "smell" to nose, from "touch" to hand, and from "taste" to mouth.

### Matching Senses
Draw a line from the eye to the child using binoculars, from the ear to the child using headphones, from the nose to the child smelling flowers, from the mouth to the child eating watermelon, and from the hand to the child petting a dog.

### pp. 110–111
### Where Are They?
The stick bug is **on** the stick. The owl is **in** the tree. The fox is **on** the snow. The deer is **behind** the tree.

### Count Me In!
I see 3 elephants. I see 5 meerkats. I see 4 zebras. I see 6 flamingos.

### pp. 112–113
### Who's Who?
Circle shoes and glue.

### A Sweet Tweet
Circle the leaf and bee.

### And Now, Meow
Circle the cow, cloud, and owl.

### pp. 114–115
### Quiet or Not Quiet?
The howling dog goes next in the first pattern, and the howling monkey goes next in the second pattern.

### Noisy Animals
The lion, monkey, and bird are making noise.

### pp. 116–117
### Big and Loud

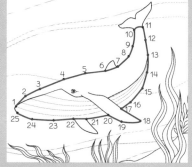

### Code Breaker
Blue whale

### Which Is Loudest?
Circle the gorilla.

### pp. 118–119
### Feeling Your Way

## Soft or Hard
The cat, dandelion, and sheep are soft; the rock, pine cone, and seashell are hard.

## pp. 120–121
### Hot or Cold?
The ice cream, ice cube, and ice pop are cold.
### What's It Like Outside?
Place an *H* next to the top right and bottom left photos, and a *C* next to the top left and bottom right photos.

## pp. 122–123
### I Know a Rhyme
Circle the hose, toes, and bows.
### I Need a Nose!

## pp. 124–125
### Smelly Sorting
Circle the flower and strawberry. Cross out the garbage and skunk.
### R as in Rose!
Circle the raccoon, rabbit, and rhino.

## pp. 126–127
### What's for Lunch?
Draw a line from the seal to the fish, from the bird to the seeds, from the caterpillar to the leaf, and from the panda to the bamboo.

## A Taste of the Garden
There are 3 pumpkins, 5 heads of lettuce, 10 ears of corn, 9 carrots, and 6 tomatoes.

## pp. 128–129
### Wonderful Whiskers
Circle the cat and seal.
### Awesome Antennae
Circle the grasshopper and butterfly.
### How Do You Feel?

# Chapter 6: Bugs and Friends
## pp. 134–135
### All About A
Draw lines from *A* to the alligator, axe, ambulance, and apple.
### 6 Legs
Circle the ant, butterfly, dung beetle, and fly.

## p. 136
### Busy Bee

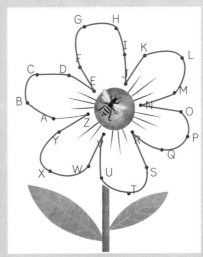

## pp. 138–139
### Beetles Big and Small
Circle the Hercules beetle, and put a square around the carrion beetle. Circle the stag beetle, and draw a square around the weevil.
### Find Your Way, Beetle!

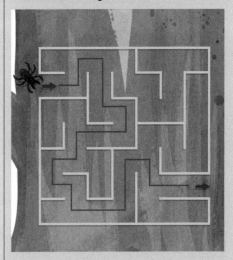

## pp. 140–141
### Spot It
$7 + 2 = 9$; $3 + 4 = 7$
### Snug as a Bug
Circle the rug and mug.
### Which Lady Comes Next?
The ladybug with its wings spread comes next in the pattern.

## p. 143
### Get It in Order
The correct order written on the lines from top to bottom is 1, 4, 2, 3.

## pp. 144–145
### Inching Along
Circle the paper clip in the top row, and circle the nail in the bottom row.

## Marigold Code

### pp. 146–147

**Who's Next?**
The black spider comes next in the pattern.

**Look-Alike Webs**

### pp. 148–149

**Color Me Beautiful**
Draw a line from the giraffe weevil to red, from the butterfly to yellow, from the mint beetle to blue, and from the praying mantis to green.

**Fliers and Crawlers**

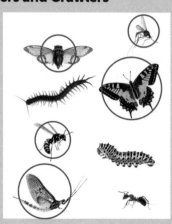

### pp. 150–151
**Write It, Picture It**

**D Is for Dragonfly**
Draw lines from *D* to the duck, dolphin, dog, and deer.

### pp. 152–153

**Fly Away Rhyme**
Circle the pie, tie, eye, and sky.

**So Many Fireflies**
10 + 3 = 13; 6 + 5 = 11; 8 + 4 = 12

### pp. 154–155

**Champion Jumper**
Circle the middle grasshopper. It jumped the farthest.

**Alphabet Hop**

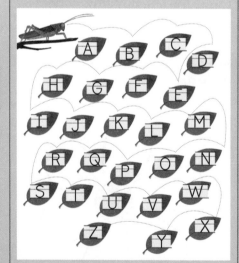

### pp. 156–157

**Crawly Collections**
The scientist needs 2 more insects.

## Syllable Counting
Circle the bee, ant, and moth in the top half. Circle the grasshopper, butterfly, and ladybug in the bottom half. There are 4 syllables in "caterpillar."

### p. 159
**Find Those Bugs**

| A | N | T | B | X | S |
|---|---|---|---|---|---|
| W | C | O | E | G | P |
| O | M | K | E | S | I |
| R | F | L | Y | H | D |
| M | O | T | H | U | E |
| G | H | Z | J | Q | R |

# Chapter 7: Baby Animals
### pp. 162–163

**Find My Mom**
Draw a line from the hen to its chick, from the elephant to its calf, from the robin to its hatchlings, and from the cow to its calf.

**Is Baby In or On?**
The puppy is **in** its house. The kitten is **on** the pillow. The fish are **in** the tank. The penguin is **on** the snow.

### pp. 164–165

**Playful Cubs**
There are 2 bear cubs.

**So Many Prints**
The top line has 6 paw prints; the middle has 12 paw prints; and the bottom has 9 paw prints.

**Playtime Favorites**
t**o**p, b**a**t, n**e**t, k**i**te, g**a**mes, c**u**be

## pp. 166–167

**How Many Ears?**
The foxes have 4 ears.

**Listen for the Fox**
Circle the box, rocks, blocks, and socks.

## pp. 168–169

**Dinnertime!**
There are 13 fish.

**A Real Meal for a Seal**
Circle the wheel.

**Counting Steps**
The missing numbers are 7 and 9.

## pp. 170–171

**More Bamboo?**
There are 7 bamboo stalks. There are not enough in the top. Draw 3 more stalks.

**A Changing Cub**
The new words are "cup" and "pup."

## p. 172

**Clap and Count**
"Strawberry" has 3 syllables; "apple" has 2 syllables; "tomato" has 3 syllables; "banana" has 3 syllables; "egg" has 1 syllable; "corn" has 1 syllable.

## pp. 174–175

**All Grown Up**
Draw a line from the top left to middle right, from the middle left to bottom right, and from the bottom left to top right.

**How Many Are Left?**
There are 5 butterflies left. There are 2 ladybugs left. There are 2 frogs left.

## pp. 176–177

**Who Has More?**
The puppy on the right has more bones. The kitten on the left has more balls of yarn.

**Funny Bunny Math**

## pp. 178–179

**Rhyming Riddle**
There will be 5 ducklings. The key and tree rhyme with "see" and "be."

**Picture Riddle**
There are 8 *V*'s.

## pp. 180–181

**Z as in Zebra**
Circle the zero and zipper.

**E as in Elephant**
Circle the egg.

**Tall, Taller, Tallest**
Circle the giraffe on the left, and draw a line under the giraffe on the right.

# Chapter 8: Dino Days
## pp. 188–189
**Dino Dots**

**High Fliers**
Circle the dinosaur holding the number 27.

## pp. 190–191

**A Dino Beginning**
Place check marks next to the tree, turtle, and tooth.

**A Dino Ending**
Place check marks next to the box, fox, and axe.

## pp. 192–193

**Hidden Dino Words**

| P | T | O | O | T | H | S |
|---|---|---|---|---|---|---|
| G | B | H | K | E | G | C |
| H | O | R | N | P | N | A |
| A | N | L | E | G | I | L |
| C | E | C | L | A | W | E |

**Parts and Pieces**
The words in the top row, from left to right, should be "back," "neck," and "eye." The words in the bottom row, from left to right, should be "tail," "leg," and "mouth."

## pp. 194–195
### Find My Kind

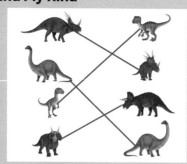

### Staying Together

## pp. 196–197
### Addition Party
4 + 3 = 7; 2 + 4 = 6.

### Snack Time
There are 6 leaves left in the top group. There are 4 leaves left in the bottom group.

## pp. 198–199
### Listen for the E
Circle the bed, ten, pen, and legs.

### Colorful Sounds
Circle red and yellow.

### Race to the Nest

## pp. 200–201
### Number Sizes
The missing numbers in the top diagonal row are 11, 12, 13. The missing numbers in the bottom diagonal row are 14, 15, 16.

### Record Breaker

## p. 202
### Starting Sounds
Circle stick, star, stairs, and stage.

## pp. 204–205
### Fossil Count
There are 2 leg bones, 2 teeth, and 3 skulls. There are total of 7 fossils.

### Dino Eggs
There are 10 groups of 10.

## pp. 206–207
### Fossil Matchup
Draw a line from the top left to the middle right, from the middle left to bottom right, and from the bottom left to top right.

### Grouping Game

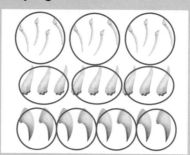

## p. 208
### Check It Out
Circle *All About Dinos*. Underline Shruti Aggarwal.

## p. 211
### Dino-Mazing

## Chapter 9: On the Move
## pp. 214–215
### Transportation Scramble
"bike," "bus," "car," "boat"

### Where Does It Go?
Draw a line from the top left to third right, from the second left to top right, from the third left to bottom right, and from bottom left to second right.

## p. 216
### Puzzles That Go

|   | ¹B |   |   |
|---|---|---|---|
|   | U |   | ³P |
| ²S | H | I | P |
|   |   |   | L |
| | ⁵C | | A |
| ⁴T | R | A | I | N |
|   | R |   | E |

## pp. 218–219

**The Shape of a Wheel**
Circle the clock. It is the same shape as a wheel.

**A Parade of Wheels**
There are 15 wheels.

## pp. 220–221

**Vehicle Rhymes**
1."Boat" and "float"; 2. "car" and "far"; 3. "truck" and "stuck"; 4."us" and "bus."

**Vehicle Names**

"Train" and "plane" rhyme.

## pp. 222–223

**Traffic Tally**
There are 3 buses, 4 trucks, and 7 cars.

**Out of a Jam**

## p. 224

**Vehicle Opposites**
Draw a line from big to small, from fast to slow, and from over to under.

## pp. 226–227

**To the Ice-Cream Shop!**
A square comes next in the top row, and a circle comes next in the bottom row.

**The Wheels on the Bikes**
10 wheels on red bikes; 8 wheels on blue bikes; 10 + 8 = 18

## p. 228

**On the Tracks**
The missing numbers are 91, 92, 93, 94, 95, 96, 97, 98, 99.

## pp. 230–231

**Fast Cars**
Circle the car going 71 miles per hour. It is going the fastest.

**Faster or Slower?**
The plane will go faster. The bike will go slower. The bus will go faster.

## pp. 232–233

**Working Trucks**

**Rock Pickup**
Groups of 4 circled rocks will vary. There are 5 groups.

## pp. 234–235

**F as in Fire Truck**
Circle the fish, frog, and flower.

**Who's the Helper?**

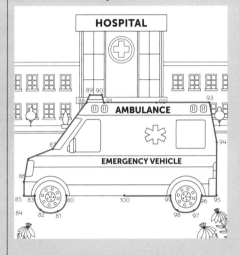

## pp. 236–237

**Pretty Balloons**
The balloon with the purple vertical stripes goes next in the top row. The polka-dot balloon goes next in the middle row. The balloon with the dog goes next in the bottom row.

**Where to Next?**

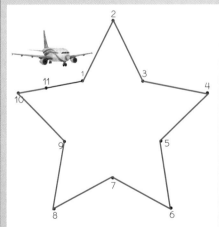

# Skills Index

Use the index to find the activities that can give your child practice with letters, math, reading, writing, and early concepts such as science, colors, and sorting.

## Early Concepts

*The Early Concepts skill category has been divided into the following categories.*

### Colors
20 – Around the Globe
43 – A Splash of Color!
45 – Color Me Perfect!
69 – Scorpion Shapes
82 – Red Shirt, Blue Shirt
94 – Refill the Paint Tray
95 – Paint by Number
145 – Marigold Code
148 – Color Me Beautiful
158 – My Butterfly Pal
195 – Staying Together

### Drawing
29 – Be an Explorer
53 – Keep Learning!
79 – Survival Hero
97 – Shapes and More Shapes
98 – Scoop It Up
104 – Your Turn
123 – I Need a Nose!
130–131 – Picture It!
146 – Give Me Legs!
150 – Write It, Picture It
156 – Crawly Collections
170 – More Bamboo?
171 – A Changing Cub
173 – My Favorite Food
182 – My Favorite Baby
183 – Baby Me
209 – Your Turn
210 – Dino Favorites
217 – What Moves?
238 – That's Me!
239 – Dream Trip

### Life Skills
59 – Ready for the Journey
91 – Reading a Recipe
120 – Hot or Cold?
231 – Faster or Slower?

### Mazes
19 – Reef Maze
33 – The Search for Figs
77 – Go Home, Penguin!
99 – Find the Party!
118 – Feeling Your Way
139 – Find Your Way, Beetle!
199 – Race to the Nest
211 – Dino-Mazing
223 – Out of a Jam

### Patterns
12 – Pretty Patterns
97 – Shapes and More Shapes
114 – Quiet or Not Quiet?
117 – Code Breaker
141 – Which Lady Comes Next?
145 – Marigold Code
146 – Who's Next?
226 – To the Ice-Cream Shop!
236 – Pretty Balloons

### Position Words
13 – Find the Corals
36 – Where Am I?
56 – Spot the Animals
110 – Where Are They?
163 – Is Baby In or On?

### Science
20 – Around the Globe
29 – Be an Explorer
39 – In the Night Sky
53 – Keep Learning!
74 – Plants All Around
78 – What Lives There?
79 – Survival Hero
108 – Bear Sense
126 – What's for Lunch?
130–131 – Picture It!
162 – Find My Mom
174 – All Grown Up
193 – Parts and Pieces

### Sorting, Matching, and Ordering
23 – Which One Belongs?
24 – Big or Small?
39 – Day and Night!
39 – In the Night Sky
43 – A Splash of Color!
47 – What Happens Next?
58 – Hold That Water
59 – Ready for the Journey
61 – Shadow Match
63 – "X" It Out
70 – Size Wise
74 – Plants All Around
76 – Tell About It
78 – What Lives There?
91 – Reading a Recipe
93 – Sort the Supplies
96 – Flat or Solid?
100 – Ball Count
102 – Budding Buddies
108 – Bear Sense
109 – Matching Senses
115 – Noisy Animals
117 – Which Is Loudest?
119 – Soft or Hard?
120 – Hot or Cold?
121 – What's It Like Outside?
124 – Smelly Sorting
126 – What's for Lunch?
128 – Wonderful Whiskers
129 – Awesome Antennae
135 – 6 Legs
138 – Beetles Big and Small
143 – Get It in Order
147 – Look-Alike Webs
148 – Color Me Beautiful
149 – Fliers and Crawlers
154 – Champion Jumper
162 – Find My Mom
174 – All Grown Up
181 – Tall, Taller, Tallest
194 – Find My Kind
206 – Fossil Matchup
215 – Where Does It Go?
224 – Vehicle Opposites
232 – Working Trucks

### Letters
8 – A is for Angelfish
11 – Ready to Pop!
11 – B is for Bubbles
12 – C is for Coral
14 – D is for Dolphin
16 – E is for Eel
18 – F is for Fish
19 – Reef Maze
21 – G is for Globe
22 – H is for Humpback
25 – I is for Isopod
26 – J is for Jellyfish
32 – K is for Kinkajou
33 – The Search for Figs
34 – L is for Lemur
35 – Rainforest Friends
36 – Where Am I?
36 – M is for Monkey
38 – N is for Nighttime
39 – Day and Night!
40 – O is for Okapi
42 – P is for Parrot
44 – Q is for Quetzal
45 – Color Me Perfect!
46 – R is for Rain
48 – What Begins With S?
48 – S is for Snake
49 – Snake Shapes
50 – T is for Tree Frog
56 – U is for Under
58 – V is for Very Hot!
60 – W is for Wonder
63 – X is in Excellent!
64 – Y is for Yucca
66 – Z is for Zigzag
66 – Catch Some Z's
68 – What's That Creature?
75 – Joshua Tree
83 – Letter the Way
96 – Flat or Solid?
99 – Find the Party!
101 – Ready to Climb
103 – Along the Garden Path
121 – What's It Like Outside?
129 – How Do You Feel?
136 – Busy Bee
137 – Flower Power
145 – Marigold Code
155 – Alphabet Hop
165 – Playtime Favorites
179 – Picture Riddle
187 – Get to Know Them
190 – A Dino Beginning
191 – A Dino Ending
201 – Record Breaker
211 – Dino-Mazing
234 – F as in Fire Truck

## Math

8 – Time to Eat!
9 – Find the One
10 – Double Bubble
13 – See the Clownfish!
14 – Nosedive!
16 – Fab Fives
17 – Wiggly Fives
18 – Fish Find
21 – Hidden Turtles
22 – Feeding Time!
24 – Big or Small?
25 – Big Sharks
26 – 10 Tentacles
27 – What's Hiding?
32 – A Fig Feast
37 – A Monkey Meal
41 – Leaf Math
42 – Sticking Together
47 – What Happens Next?
50 – Fly, Fly, Fly!
57 – Stay Cool!
65 – How Many Leaves?
67 – Home Sweet Home
69 – Scorpion Shapes
70 – Size Wise
73 – Do the Math
82 – Red Shirt, Blue Shirt
86 – Jump to It!
87 – Time to Share
89 – It's a Pizza Pie
89 – A Piece of Pizza, Please!
90 – It's Raining Raisins!
95 – Paint by Number
96 – Flat or Solid?
97 – Shapes and More Shapes
98 – Scoop It Up
100 – Ball Count
111 – Count Me In!
116 – Big and Loud
127 – A Taste of the Garden
135 – 6 Legs
140 – Spot It
144 – Inching Along
146 – Give Me Legs!
153 – So Many Fireflies
156 – Crawly Collections
157 – Syllable Counting
164 – Playful Cubs
164 – So Many Prints
166 – How Many Ears?
168 – Dinnertime!
169 – Counting Steps
170 – More Bamboo?
172 – Clap and Count
175 – How Many Are Left?
176 – Who Has More?
177 – Funny Bunny Math
178 – Rhyming Riddle
188 – Dino Dots
189 – High Fliers
196 – Addition Party
197 – Snack Time
200 – Number Sizes
204 – Fossil Count
205 – Dino Eggs
207 – Grouping Game
218 – The Shape of a Wheel
219 – A Parade of Wheels
222 – Traffic Tally
226 – To the Ice-Cream Shop!
227 – The Wheels on the Bikes
228 – On the Tracks
230 – Fast Cars
233 – Rock Pickup
235 – Who's the Helper?
237 – Where to Next?

## Reading

15 – What Starts With D?
38 – Nighttime Rhyme
40 – It's the Same Sound!
44 – Words to Know
46 – Where's the Rain?
48 – What Begins With S?
51 – Hop to It!
60 – What Does It Start With?
64 – What Can You See?
71 – Small Words
71 – Listen to the E
75 – Joshua Tree
76 – Tell About It
77 – Go Home, Penguin!
85 – B is the Best!
88 – Pick a P
91 – Reading a Recipe
92 – Oh! It's an Oboe
105 – School Words
109 – Matching Senses
112 – Who's Who?
112 – A Sweet Tweet
113 – And Now, Meow
122 – I Know a Rhyme
125 – R as in Rose
134 – All About A
137 – Flower Power
141 – Snug as a Bug
150 – Write It, Picture It!
151 – D as in Dragonfly
152 – Fly Away Rhyme
157 – Syllable Counting
159 – Find Those Bugs
163 – Is Baby In or On?
165 – Playtime Favorites
167 – Listen for the Fox
169 – A Real Meal for a Seal
171 – A Changing Cub
172 – Clap and Count
173 – Runaway Word
173 – My Favorite Food
178 – Rhyming Riddle
180 – Z as in Zebra
180 – E as in Elephant
190 – A Dino Beginning
191 – A Dino Ending
192 – Hidden Dino Words
195 – Staying Together
198 – Listen for the E
198 – Colorful Sounds
202 – Starting Sounds
203 – Trace the Plates
208 – Check It Out
214 – Transportation Scramble
217 – You Are on the Go!
220 – Vehicle Rhymes
221 – Vehicle Names
234 – F as in Fire Truck

## Writing

8 – A is for Angelfish
8 – Time to Eat!
10 – Double Bubble
11 – B is for Bubbles
12 – C is for Coral
13 – See the Clownfish!
14 – D is for Dolphin
14 – Nosedive!
16 – E is for Eel
16 – Fab Fives
18 – F is for Fish
18 – Fish Find
21 – G is for Globe
21 – Hidden Turtles
22 – Feeding Time!
22 – H is for Humpback
25 – I is for Isopod
25 – Big Sharks
26 – 10 Tentacles
26 – J is for Jellyfish
32 – K is for Kinkajou
34 – L is for Lemur
36 – M is for Monkey
38 – N is for Nighttime
39 – Day and Night!
40 – O is for Okapi
41 – Leaf Math
42 – P is for Parrot
42 – Sticking Together
44 – Words to Know
44 – Q is for Quetzal
46 – R is for Rain
47 – What Happens Next?
48 – S is for Snake
50 – T is for Tree Frog
50 – Fly, Fly, Fly!
56 – U is for Under
58 – V is for Very Hot!
60 – W is for Wonder
62 – Where's Your Home?
63 – X is in Excellent!
64 – What Can You See?
64 – Y is for Yucca
65 – How Many Leaves?
66 – Z is for Zigzag
71 – Small Words
73 – Do the Math
82 – Red Shirt, Blue Shirt
83 – Letter the Way
84 – See and Say
86 – Jump to It!
87 – Time to Share
89 – It's a Pizza Pie
90 – It's Raining Raisins!
91 – Reading a Recipe
96 – Flat or Solid?
100 – Ball Count
103 – Along the Garden Path
109 – Matching Senses
111 – Count Me In!
117 – Code Breaker
121 – What's It Like Outside?
127 – A Taste of the Garden
137 – Flower Power
140 – Spot It
143 – Get It in Order
150 – Write It, Picture It
153 – So Many Fireflies
155 – Alphabet Hop
156 – Crawly Collections
163 – Is Baby In or On?
164 – Playful Cubs
164 – So Many Prints

165 – Playtime Favorites
166 – How Many Ears?
168 – Dinnertime!
169 – Counting Steps
170 – More Bamboo?
171 – A Changing Cub
173 – Runaway Word
173 – My Favorite Food
175 – How Many Are Left?
178 – Rhyming Riddle
182 – My Favorite Baby
183 – Baby Me
187 – Get to Know Them
190 – A Dino Beginning
193 – Parts and Pieces

195 – Staying Together
196 – Addition Party
197 – Snack Time
200 – Number Sizes
203 – Trace the Plates
204 – Fossil Count
205 – Dino Eggs
209 – Your Turn
214 – Transportation Scramble
216 – Puzzles That Go
217 – You Are on the Go!
219 – A Parade of Wheels
221 – Vehicle Names
222 – Traffic Tally
225 – Work to Do

227 – The Wheels on the Bikes
228 – On the Tracks
229 – Out of Sight
233 – Rock Pickup

# Photo Credits

AS: Adobe Stock; SS: Shutterstock

COVER: polar bear illustration: Melanie Mikecz; polar bear photo: Eric Isselée/SS

1 (CTR), Eric Isselée/SS; 3 (BACKGROUND), spacezerocom/SS; 3 (LO), supparsorn/SS

CHAPTER 1 6 (CTR LE), Rich Carey/SS; 6-7 (BACKGROUND), silvae/SS; 8 (UP), Fredy Wollenstein/SS; 10 (UP), mirecca/AS; 12 (CTR), Nataliia Trushkina/SS; 12 (little coral), Volkovo/SS; 12 (big coral), Ian 2010/AS; 12 (UP), stephan kerkhofs/AS; 13 (LO RT), unterwegs/SS; 14 (UP), Photoroyalty/SS; 14 (LO), Willyam Bradberry/SS; 15 (UP LE), Allinone/SS; 15 (UP RT), nattanan726/SS; 15 (CTR LE), Passakorn Umpornmaha/SS; 15 (CTR RT), Eric Isselée/SS; 15 (LO LE), Dmitry Kalinovsky/SS; 15 (LO RT), Aksenova Natalya/SS; 16 (UP), mirecca/AS; 17 (eel), Aedka Studio/SS; 18 (CTR), Dany Kurniawan/SS; 18 (UP), Wagsy/SS; 21 (UP RT), Elnur/AS; 22 (UP), Craig Lambert Photography/SS; 23 (A), Artwizard/SS; 23 (B), gogoiso/SS; 23 (C), Namomooyim/SS; 23 (D), SiiKA Photo/SS; 23 (E), Photoongraphy/SS; 23 (F), Maks Narodenko/SS; 23 (G), Kasoga/AS; 23 (H), FocusStocker/SS; 23 (I), Lucas/AS; 23 (J), UvGroup/SS; 24 (UP), Chase Dekker/SS; 25 (UP RT), SergeUWPhoto/SS; 28 (CTR), Kryvenok Anastasiia/SS

CHAPTER 2 30-31 (BACKGROUND), worldclassphoto/SS; 30 (UP LE), apple2499/SS; 32 (UP RT), mgkuijpers/AS; 34 (UP CTR), David Havel/SS; 35 (LO RT), irin-k/SS; 35 (UP RT), cynoclub/SS; 35 (CTR RT), Vladfotograf/SS; 35 (CTR LE), Dirk Ercken/SS; 35 (UP LE), yevtushenko serhii/SS; 35 (LO LE), Eric Isselée/AS; 38 (CTR RT), IgorCheri/SS; 39 (CTR RT), Wollertz/SS; 39 (UP RT), FotoRequest/SS; 39 (LO LE), Alexandru Canpan/SS; 39 (LO RT), rahul/AS; 39 (LO CTR), Albo/AS; 39 (CTR LE), Cavan/AS; 39 (UP LE), Miguel/AS; 40 (CTR LE), Dimedrol68/SS; 40 (CTR CTR), nopparada samrhubsuk/SS; 40 (LO LE), Vereshchagin Dmitry/SS; 40 (UP RT), Eric Isselée/Dreamstime; 40 (LO RT), Eric Isselée/AS; 40 (CTR RT), robynmac/AS; 41 (UP RT), Alletah; 42 (UP RT), Nejron Photo/SS; 43 (A), Dr Ajay Kumar Singh/AS; 43 (B), julio__cc/SS; 43 (C), jdross75/AS; 43 (D), evolutionnow/AS; 43 (E), PhotocechCZ/SS; 44 (UP RT), phototrip/AS; 46 (LO CTR), canbedone/SS; 46 (LO RT), Vladimir Khodataev/SS; 46 (LO LE), ronnybas/AS; 47 (UP), SAMMYEK/SS; 47 (LO), CreativeZone/SS; 47 (CTR), makam1969/AS; 48 (A), Kay Cee Lens and Footages/SS; 48 (B), Podoplelova Irina/SS; 48 (C), Shamils/SS; 48 (D), Mathias Weil/AS; 48 (E), Torychemistry/SS; 48 (F), J-Re/SS; 48 (UP), Nynke/AS; 53 (LO RT), std_aart/SS; 53 (UP RT), Jane Rix/SS; 53 (LO CTR), LonelyStock/SS; 53 (LO LE), Lostry7/SS; 53 (UP CTR), Jan Stria/SS; 53 (UP LE), Ammit Jack/SS; 54 (LO LE), Jim/AS

CHAPTER 3 54-55 (BACKGROUND), Brent Coulter/SS; 56 (UP), Bryce Alexander/SS; 59 (LO RT), mdbildes/SS; 59 (UP RT), CH.Pirasak/SS; 59 (UP LE), Yellow Cat/SS; 59 (CTR RT), Tomasz Darul/SS; 59 (CTR LE), monticello/SS; 59 (LO LE), sagir/SS; 59 (UP RT), Nick Fox/AS; 60 (oasis), Patrick Poendl/SS; 60 (lizard), Ms.Alarika/SS; 60 (fox), Rosa Jay/SS; 60 (wing), Gallinago_media/SS; 60 (wind), Yerbolat Shadrakhov/SS; 60 (cactus), Mr Doomits/SS; 62 (LO RT), Evgeny Haritonov/SS; 62 (LO LE), Jen/AS; 63 (fish), tab62/SS; 63 (octopus), pan demin/SS; 63 (whale), Nataly23/SS; 63 (camel), mara86pred/SS; 63 (cactus), Jirapa339/SS; 63 (lizard), JDCarballo/SS; 63 (shoes),Tatevosian Yana/SS; 64 (CTR), Oleg Kovtun Hydrobio/SS; 66 (CTR CTR), Planner/SS; 66 (CTR LE), Anan Kaewkhammul/SS; 66 (LO CTR), aquariagirl1970/SS; 66 (CTR RT), Photobac/SS; 66 (UP RT), Yakov/AS; 68 (UP RT), Cyrus Matiga/SS; 69 (UP RT), Kaiskynet Studio/SS; 70 (UP RT), Charles T. Peden/SS; 72 (CTR), lightpoet/AS; 73 (camel), Alexandra Lande/SS; 73 (turtle), NickKnight/SS; 73 (cactus), Giftography/SS; 73 (snake), Eric Isselée/SS; 74 (A), photojohn830/SS; 74 (B), clayton harrison/SS; 74 (C), Ivistevie/SS; 74 (D), sumikophoto/SS; 75 (UP RT), joojoob27/SS; 75 (A), Ivaylo Ivanov/SS; 75 (B), Lucie Lang/SS; 75 (C), bestv/SS; 75 (D), Alex Staroseltsev/SS; 75 (E), masa44/SS; 75 (F), Pineapple studio/SS; 76 (UP), willtu/AS; 77 (UP RT), Kotomiti Okuma/SS; 78 (LO RT), Artorn Thongtukit/SS; 78 (LO CTR), Eric Isselée/SS; 78 (UP CTR), Tom Tietz/SS; 78 (LO LE), pan demin/SS; 78 (CTR LE), Balakleypb/SS; 78 (CTR RT), photomaster/SS; 78 (CTR CTR), Mike Price/SS

CHAPTER 4 80-81 (BACKGROUND), Andrew Angelov/SS; 83 (UP RT), feuerpferd1111/SS; 85 (UP CTR), trekandphoto/AS; 85 (CTR LE), noowans/AS; 85 (LO RT), Swapan/AS; 85 (LO CTR), Yeti Studio/AS; 85 (CTR RT), Atlas/AS; 85 (LO LE), Rawf8/AS; 87 (ball), MERCURY studio/AS; 87 (teddy bear), Nynke/AS; 87 (toy), Karana/AS; 87 (UP RT), Vladimir Prusakov/SS; 87 (UP LE), Vladimir Prusakov/SS; 88 (LO LE), Pixelbuddha Studio/AS; 88 (CTR LE), Olesia/AS; 88 (UP RT), phive2015/AS; 88 (CTR RT), Yeti Studio/AS; 88 (CTR CTR), Yeti Studio/AS; 88 (UP CTR), m.lexandrovna/AS; 88 (UP LE), kris/AS; 88 (LO RT), magann/AS; 90 (UP), Robyn Mackenzie/SS; 92 (oboe), paulmz/AS; 92 (UP LE), 4Max/AS; 92 (UP CTR), purgatory.art/AS; 92 (CTR RT), MarekPhotoDesign/AS; 92 (LO RT), BillionPhotos/AS; 92 (CTR LE), LAYER-LAB/AS; 92 (LO LE), Irina Gutyryak/AS; 92 (UP RT), benemale/AS; 93 (A), Photobeps/AS; 93 (B), Pixel-Shot/SS; 93 (C), M.Dörr & M.Frommherz/AS; 93 (D), Yuliya Karpovich/AS; 93 (E), David Pereiras/AS; 93 (F), Krakenimages/SS; 93 (G), Luciano/AS; 93 (H), stockyme/AS; 93 (I), Wolfetta/SS; 93 (J), Grafvision/AS; 94 (UP RT), New Africa/SS; 96 (UP RT), Luciano/AS; 98 (UP RT), Anastasia Turshina/SS; 100 (UP RT), karelnoppe/SS; 102 (UP CTR), David Tadevosian/SS; 105 (UP RT), Elena Elisseeva/SS

CHAPTER 5 106-107 (BACKGROUND), Alessandro Biascioli/AS; 107 (UP RT), Iakov Kalinin/SS; 109 (LE A), Olga Sapegina/SS; 109 (LE B), isara studio/SS; 109 (LE C), Dmitry-Arhangel 29/SS; 109 (LE D), binimin/AS; 109 (LE E), hxdbzxy/SS; 109 (RT A), Brostock/SS; 109 (RT B), Ann Rodchua/SS; 109 (RT C), Chot Studio/SS; 109 (RT D), Dmitry Naumov/SS; 109 (RT E), SviatlanaLaza/SS; 110 (LO RT), Wirestock Creators/SS; 110 (CTR RT), FotoRequest/SS; 110 (UP LE), Mark Brandon/SS; 110 (CTR LE), Alexey Seafarer/SS; 111 (UP LE), Stefane/AS; 111 (LO RT), Tatiana Kolosovskaya/SS; 111 (UP RT), nattanan726/SS; 111 (LO LE), tourpics_net/SS; 112 (LO LE), AlenKadr/AS; 112 (LO CTR LE), Natural PNG/AS; 112 (LO CTR RT), eak8dda/AS; 112 (UP CTR LE), Jagodka/SS; 112 (LO LE), volkova natalia/SS; 112 (UP RT), CiPariss/SS; 112 (UP CTR RT), Nynke van Holten/SS; 112 (UP LE), Angel Simon/SS; 113 (LO LE), Kay Cee Lens and Footages/SS; 113 (UP LE), neng nokom komala/SS; 113 (CTR), Sergiy1975/SS; 113 (LO RT), stockphoto-graf/SS; 113 (UP RT), Happy Together/SS; 113 (UP CTR), photomaster/SS; 114 (dog), Erik Lam/SS; 114 (monkey), Rosa Jay/SS; 114 (dog), Eric Isselée/SS; 115 (CTR LE), NataliaL/AS; 115 (CTR RT), Nilanka Sampath/SS; 115 (UP LE), Justin Dawson/SS; 115 (UP RT), BonnieBC/SS; 115 (LO RT), Linda Vos/SS; 115 (LO LE), miroslav chytil/SS; 117 (CTR LE), Vera Kuttelvaserova/AS; 117 (LO LE), fivespots/SS; 117 (LO RT), Krakenimages/SS; 118 (UP RT), Ana Prego/SS; 119 (LO RT), David Daniel/AS; 119 (CTR RT), Wirestock Collection/SS; 119 (CTR LE), KatrinSash/SS; 119 (UP RT), Bigc Studio/SS; 119 (UP LE), Borkin Vadim/SS; 119 (LO RT), ismailGazel/SS; 120 (CTR CTR), grey/AS; 120 (CTR RT), Anna_Pustynnikova/SS; 120 (UP RT), Pixel-Shot/SS; 120 (LO LE), MaraZe/SS; 120 (LO RT), baibaz/SS; 120 (CTR LE), M. Unal Ozmen/SS; 121 (LO RT), ezp/AS; 121 (UP RT), Guas/SS; 121 (LO LE), Altug Galip/SS; 121 (CTR RT), JulezHohlfeld/SS; 121 (CTR LE), Andrei Stepanov/SS; 122 (UP LE), schankz/SS; 122 (CTR RT), Boris Sosnovyy/SS; 122 (CTR LE), Drakuliren/SS; 122 (LO RT), Eric Isselée/SS; 122 (UP RT), Licvin/SS; 122 (LO LE), stacy2010ua/SS; 122 (CTR CTR), TaniaKitura/SS; 124 (LO CTR), Nynke/AS; 124 (CTR RT), Iurii Kachkovskyi/AS; 124 (CTR CTR), beboy/SS; 124 (UP RT), fizkes/SS; 124 (CTR LE), Mega Pixel/SS; 125 (CTR RT), Jiang Hongyan/SS; 125 (UP), Lotus Images/SS; 125 (CTR LE), HYLE/SS; 125 (LO LE), VladyslaV Travel photo/SS; 125 (UP RT), Eric Isselée/SS; 125 (UP LE), Anan Kaewkhammul/SS; 126 (UP), LumenSt/SS; 126 (LE A), Dolores M. Harvey/SS; 126 (LE B), EwaStudio/AS; 126 (LE C),Darkdiamond67/SS; 126 (LE D), Saqib alii/SS; 126 (RT A), Valentina Razumova/SS; 126 (RT B), Tim UR/SS; 126 (RT C), JGade/SS; 126 (RT D), CeltStudio/SS;128 (UP RT), abet/AS; 128 (LO LE), Sandra Standbridge/AS; 128 (CTR RT), Nagova87/SS; 128 (UP LE), Henner Damke/SS; 128 (LO RT), Matthew Gordon/SS; 128 (CTR LE), nataliatamkovich/SS; 129 (UP RT), Hardi/AS; 129 (LO RT), rima15/AS; 129 (UP CTR RT), LedyX/SS; 129 (UP LE), Ernie Cooper/SS; 129 (UP CTR LE), RT Images/SS; 130 (UP RT), Eric Isselée/SS

CHAPTER 6 132-133 (BACKGROUND), murgvi/AS; 134 (UP RT), xiaoliangge/AS; 134 (LO RT), Maks Narodenko/AS; 134 (LO LE), luisalealmelo/AS; 134 (CTR LE), Henner Damke/SS; 134 (CTR RT), F8 studio/SS; 134 (UP CTR), Svetlana Foote/SS; 134 (UP LE), Artem Kutsenko/SS; 135 (LE A), SKphotographer/AS; 135 (LE B), 127233251/SS; 135 (LE C), SKphotographer/SS; 135 (LE D), MakroBetz/SS; 135 (RT A), Charles Brutlag/SS; 135 (RT B), anatchant/AS; 135 (RT C), creativenature/AS; 135 (RT D), Aleksandar Dickov/SS; 138 (LO LE), Fyle/AS; 138 (UP LE), Anton/AS; 138 (UP CTR), Mark Brandon/SS; 138 (UP LE), Ernie Cooper/SS; 138 (UP LE), Wirestock Creators/SS; 138 (LO RT), Pavel Jakubec/SS; 141 (UP RT), mehmetkrc/AS; 141 (ladybug), Chepko Danil/SS; 141 (A), gromovataya/AS; 141 (B), Dima Moroz/SS; 141 (C), vitaliy_73/SS; 141 (D), Yulik_art/SS; 141 (E), LittlePerfectStock/SS; 141 (F), Kabardins photo/SS; 141, New Africa/SS; 143 (A), Breck P. Kent/SS; 143 (B), mramsdell1967/AS; 143 (C), Betty Rong/AS; 143 (B), rabbitti/AS; 144 (LO CTR), modify260/AS; 144 (UP LE), zhang yongxin/AS; 144 (CTR LE), xy/AS; 144 (UP RT), Thijs de Graaf/SS; 144 (LO LE), Dan Kosmayer/AS; 144 (LO RT), Panupong786/SS; 144 (CTR CTR), domnitsky/SS; 144 (CTR RT),

# On an Adventure

**Think of the place you'd most like to visit in the world. Draw a picture of yourself there.**

# NATIONAL GEOGRAPHIC KiDS

Turn the page for your Explorer Award!

# Explorer Award

## Great job!

You learned all about the wide world around you. You are ready for an amazing adventure!

**This award goes to:**

_____

_____

**Write your name on the line.**